Birdfeeder
Garden

RSPB

Birdfeeder Garden

ROBERT BURTON

DORLING KINDERSLEY
LONDON • NEW YORK • SYDNEY • MOSCOW

A DORLING KINDERSLEY BOOK

Produced for Dorling Kindersley by PAGE*One*
Cairn House, Elgiva Lane, Chesham,
Buckinghamshire HP5 2JD

PROJECT DIRECTORS Bob Gordon and Helen Parker
EDITOR Charlotte Stock
DESIGNER Matthew Cook

SENIOR MANAGING EDITOR Krystyna Mayer
MANAGING ART EDITOR Philip Gilderdale
PRODUCTION CONTROLLER Antony Heller
PICTURE RESEARCHERS Sam Ward and Victoria Walker

First published in Great Britain in 1998
by Dorling Kindersley Limited,
9 Henrietta Street, London WC2E 8PS

A CIP catalogue record for this book
is available from the British Library

ISBN 0-7513-0440-9

Reproduced by Bright Arts, Hong Kong
Printed and bound in Singapore by
Star Standard Industries

CONTENTS

FOREWORD 6

INTRODUCTION 8

Chapter One
LANDSCAPING FOR BIRDS

FOREWORD

THOSE WHO ARE FAMILIAR with the nature books of Richard Jefferies will know that he wrote mostly about the countryside of North Wiltshire in the United Kingdom as he knew it a century ago. When I first discovered Jefferies in the 1940s, that landscape and wildlife were still much as he described it. Today, I cannot read him without a deep sense of loss. This short passage speaks for itself:

> *"Our English landscape wants no gardening: it cannot be gardened. The least interference kills it. The beauty of English woodland and country is in its detail. There is nothing empty and unclothed. If the clods are left a little while undisturbed in the fields, weeds spring up and wild flowers bloom upon them… . Never was there a garden like the meadow: there is not an inch of the meadow in the early summer without a flower."*
> RICHARD JEFFERIES, "AN ENGLISH DEER PARK", *FIELD AND HEDGEROW*, 1889

I am writing this foreword only a few miles from Jefferies's old home at Coate in Wiltshire and it is early summer. In the meadows where I walked this morning, there was scarcely a flower to be seen. So thoroughly are the fields now 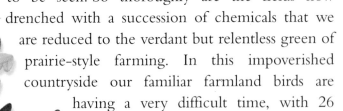 drenched with a succession of chemicals that we are reduced to the verdant but relentless green of prairie-style farming. In this impoverished countryside our familiar farmland birds are having a very difficult time, with 26 species in serious decline and others struggling to hold their own. In the worst cases, the populations have crashed by almost 90 per cent. Sadly, the same story is repeated throughout the world, wherever there is intensification and urbanization.

If the situation is retrievable – and in my view it is a very big *if* – it will need urgent action by institutions and by individuals. This is not the place to discuss what governments need to do, but every one of us, particularly if we have a garden, can play a role and make a valuable contribution.

It has often been pointed out that the total area of gardens in the United Kingdom far exceeds the combined acreage of all our nature reserves. In this huge and varied patchwork of cultivation, both in our towns and in the countryside, there is immense potential for helping wildlife. I say "potential" because gardens can only be really beneficial if they are managed with wildlife in mind. If they are not, they can be as barren and unfriendly as any agricultural business that is run solely for profit.

BIRDFEEDER GARDEN is directed, of course, to those who wish to create a garden that will attract birds. It cannot unfortunately help all farmland birds because there are some species that will never find the right conditions to breed and feed in your garden, however cleverly it is managed. But you can provide a haven for many of the threatened species and by doing so you will benefit a wide variety of other life: plants, butterflies, amphibians, reptiles, and small mammals.

Richard Jefferies wrote: "*The beauty of English woodland and country is in its detail*". Now that much of that detail has been removed, you have the opportunity, with the help of this excellent book, to restore some colour and variety to the scene.

JULIAN PETTIFER
RSPB President

INTRODUCTION

BIRDFEEDER GARDEN combines the popular pursuits of gardening and birdfeeding to create a garden that can be enjoyed for its horticultural and wildlife interest. The book explores ways of bringing the appeal of birds' natural habitats into your garden to encourage a variety of bird species to feed, nest, and shelter during the year.

The Disappearing Countryside

Over the last 50 years, undeveloped rural areas have been modified or destroyed at an alarming rate. Woods, grasslands, marshes, and ponds have been replaced by housing and industrial

Following the Plough
Open farmland is a natural habitat of birds, providing them with a year-round source of seeds and insects, as well as shelter and nesting sites.

Haven for Birds
Whatever its size, a garden can be adapted to offer the types of food and shelter that attract birds in their natural habitats (see opposite).

developments. Farmland sadly reflects the changes in agricultural practice such as the removal of hedgerows and the chemical control of pests and weeds, both of which have robbed birds of valuable shelter and food. The rapid disappearance of natural habitats stresses the urgency and importance of the role that bird gardens can play in wildlife conservation. Together with urban squares, parks, golf courses, and reservoirs, gardens are becoming important refuges for many bird species that can no longer survive in the countryside.

You can encourage birds into your garden by recreating certain features that they prefer in their natural habitats. There is no doubt that birdfeeding helps many birds to survive crop failures or spells of severe weather, when snow and frost lock up natural foods and starvation threatens. Birdfeeding also helps to maintain a high population for species that only overwinter in gardens. These birds return to the countryside to nest in spring, but since more of them have been able to survive the winter, they nest earlier, and raise more young.

A New Style of Gardening

Gardening for birds must be a positive action, based on a layout and planting scheme that have been well thought out. Neglecting the garden in the hope that it will become "wild" produces nothing more than an unkempt mess of unwanted plants that are of little value to birds. Equally, an extremely well-manicured garden can be even less successful because the insects, seeds, and fruits that attract birds are eliminated by overzealous weeding, pruning, pest control, and general tidying. Some studies of birds have shown that fewer young are produced in gardens than in the countryside because of a shortage of food for nestlings.

The challenge for bird gardeners is to try to balance horticultural excellence with the provision of what birds need. The first step to becoming a truly successful bird gardener is to learn about the nesting and feeding habits of the species that are likely to visit your garden. Ornithological research into the lives and ecology of garden birds enables us to assess their seasonal requirements and to remedy any deficiencies in their habitats. Drawing birds into your garden involves more than occasionally scattering bread crusts and kitchen scraps during the winter months. It is a year-round cycle of providing the right food at the right time, ensuring that plenty of cover is available for nesting or shelter, and supplying a source of fresh water for drinking and bathing. Your bird visitors will also need protection from nest robbers and other predators.

Imitating a Natural Habitat
A wide range of native plants that are found in the countryside can be grown in the birdfeeder's garden. They all provide natural food for birds and are adapted to suit the local soil type, climate, and location. In addition to the plants suggested in this book, you may find other examples, including exotic or ornamental specimens, that can be used to enhance the horticultural and visual interest of your garden.

Bear in mind that there is no guarantee of a certain bird species visiting your garden even if you have grown plants that are known to be attractive to this species. Alder cones are an important food for siskins, but these birds will visit an alder tree in your garden only if they are already in the vicinity. They will, no doubt, also visit your peanut feeder but it is much more interesting to watch them feeding on one of their natural foods. Plants are especially important for attracting birds that do not come to birdfeeders. For example, bullfinches feed on clover and dandelion seeds found on a garden lawn, but ignore feeders full of peanuts and sunflower seeds that may be hanging overhead.

Stalks and Stems
Many of the plants enjoyed by birds in their natural habitats can be grown among tall grasses in a wildflower garden. They are good sources of insects for birds such as reed buntings.

A Pleasure to Watch
As well as being a sanctuary for birds, the bird garden hosts a spectacle of colours, songs, and bustling activity. Bird gardening can develop into a consuming hobby. When a new bird species appears in your garden, it can be as rewarding as raising a new variety of plant. When designing your bird garden or siting a birdtable, take into account any vantage points from where the daily comings and goings of your bird visitors can be observed.

Mutual Benefits

One mixed blessing for the bird gardener is that birds eat many of the insects and small animals that frequently become garden pests, especially in vegetable plots. The drawback to this form of pest control is that birds will also help themselves to your fruits and flowers. Birds such as blue tits are a positive help when they feed caterpillars and aphids to their young, but they are less welcome when they peck at gooseberries or currants, raid pea pods, and ruthlessly strip fruit blossoms. While the loss of your carefully nurtured crops may make you despondent at first, the many positive aspects of bird gardening easily outweigh such a setback.

Whatever the size of your garden, be it a large, rambling pasture, paved courtyard or terrace, or just a couple of windowboxes, you can make a personal contribution to wildlife conservation. Creating a bird garden is a practical and affordable project in which everyone, whatever their gardening skills, can and should be encouraged to take part.

Hidden Food
The acrobatic manoeuvres of blue tits can often be seen in flowering fruit trees. The birds search the blossoms for insects hidden inside and sometimes sip the nectar.

Watering Point
All birds need access to water for drinking and bathing. Water birds such as moorhens may even nest in your garden if there is a large pond nearby. They will use a selection of twigs and dead reeds to build their nests.

Chapter One

LANDSCAPING FOR BIRDS

VARIETY IS THE KEY to a successful garden and this is especially true for bird gardens. Whatever its size, your garden can draw a greater range and number of birds throughout the year if it is landscaped and planted with the needs of birds in mind. While a large or mature garden offers more scope for attracting birds, a small or new garden can be just as rewarding, if some preliminary thought is given to its layout.

Every bird is looking for the necessities of life that it would expect to find in its natural habitat, namely food, water, and shelter. This chapter presents ideas and practical suggestions on how to design, construct, or enhance a birdfeeder's garden that offers these essential services for as many species of bird as possible.

Gardening to attract and cater for birds adds an extra dimension to gardens that are managed purely for their horticultural value, and will bring you pleasure and excitement as a gardener and birdwatcher alike.

Visiting Magpie
A well-established pond and bog garden attracts many garden birds, which drink, bathe, and often feed on the resident and visiting wildlife.

BIRDS AND PLANTS

THE PLANTING SCHEME chosen for your garden influences the number and type of birds that will be encouraged to visit. In general, the greater the variety and quantity of plants, the better your garden caters for the necessities of bird life. Plants provide food in the form of fruits, seeds, and buds, while their foliage offers shelter and nesting material.

Fruits and Seeds

Two of the most important sources of food for birds are fruits and seeds. Some plants rely on animals, especially birds, for seed dispersal. These plants package their seeds in fruits that offer nutritious flesh in a coloured outer skin, which is designed to attract hungry visitors. Once eaten, the seeds may be deposited, at a distance from the parent plant, in droppings

Hawthorn
As well as providing winter berries for birds, hawthorn has dense, thorny foliage that offers well-protected nesting sites.

Leaves are used as nest material

Some birds strip blossom

Plump, fleshy fruits filled with seeds

Gooseberry
Gooseberries that are left to ripen on the bush attract birds. The large, succulent fruits are swallowed whole by blackbirds.

Angelica
The large sprays of white or pink angelica flowers attract insects, which provide food for blue tits and greenfinches during summer. The seeds are encased in winged fruits and are eaten by birds in autumn and winter (see p. 117).

Flowerheads are good source of seeds in autumn

Flowers are produced in multi-spoked sprays

Hollow stem

Protective sheath-base

that make rich fertilizers. Other seeds, such as sticky mistletoe seeds, are distributed when birds wipe their beaks against branches after eating the plant's berries. Some birds, such as blackbirds and robins, commonly regurgitate a mass of seeds in an action called "heaving".

Fruits advertise their edibility by the colour of their skins. Most of them mature to black or red to show that they are ripe. Red contrasts very strongly with green foliage while black, a less obvious contrast, reflects ultraviolet light, which is visible to birds but not to us. White fruits are generally not very attractive to birds. The size of fruits is also important. Small berries, such as elder and cotoneaster, are easy for the smallest of birds to eat, but larger fruits can present difficulties. Blackbirds are large enough to pluck the fruits of cherry laurels, while the smaller song thrushes have to hang from the fruits to tear them free, and tits can only take small pieces of flesh from large fruits.

Garden Creatures

Plants provide a secondary source of food for birds in the form of insects, spiders, and small animals, such as slugs and snails, that feed on them. Insects are especially important during the nesting season since they provide most garden birds, even some renowned seed-eaters, such as finches, with food for their newly hatched young. In particular, nuthatches, tits, great spotted woodpeckers, and warblers rely on caterpillars to feed their nestlings.

To date, little research has been made into identifying the best sources of insects for garden birds. It is generally best to plant native species since these will attract local insects that have adapted to feed on them, whereas garden varieties are often resistant to insects. The more foliage produced in your garden – whether on trees, shrubs, herbaceous plants, or weeds – the more insects will be attracted. A well-kept, weed-free garden, where cultivated plants are kept neat and tidy and old growth is trimmed and cut away, will not support a broad variety or large populations of insects. Birds will

Food for Nestlings
Blue tits can often be seen feeding on aphids, which are an important food for nestlings in the summer.

benefit more if you let your garden become slightly unkempt, leaving flowerheads to seed, allowing plants to sprawl, and using pesticides and chemical treatments as little as possible.

Birds and Shelter

Trees and shrubs provide birds with safe places for roosting and nesting. Even a shrub with bare branches offers some night-time shelter for birds and can make all the difference in cold weather. Regular pruning and trimming of trees and shrubs encourages a dense branch structure and thick foliage which, together with plants cloaked in needles or spines, will be welcomed by small birds as a refuge from attack by predators. Again, an untidy garden harbouring plenty of undergrowth is the best environment for birds looking for shelter. You can also supplement the natural nesting and roosting sites in your garden by providing nestboxes, tree hollows, and artificial thickets.

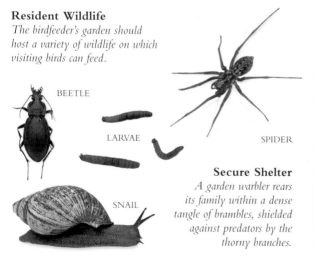

Resident Wildlife
The birdfeeder's garden should host a variety of wildlife on which visiting birds can feed.

BEETLE

LARVAE

SPIDER

SNAIL

Secure Shelter
A garden warbler rears its family within a dense tangle of brambles, shielded against predators by the thorny branches.

PLANNING A GARDEN

WHILE A BIRDFEEDER'S GARDEN caters for a very specific set of occupants, it should also be pleasing to you. If gardening is not your favourite pastime, then opt for a design that needs little maintenance. Before introducing any changes to your existing garden, carry out routine maintenance for a year, while you discover what it contains – making the right decisions at this stage may save expensive corrections later. Temporary improvements can be made with annuals, bedding plants, or even shrubs, which can be carefully moved later on.

FILLING IN THE DETAILS

Once you have decided on your garden layout, you can start to add in the details of new features and plants.

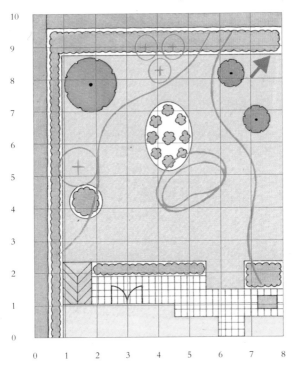

DRAWING UP A PLAN

Using squared paper, make a scale drawing of the garden's basic framework. Take photographs or make sketches to help your memory. Look at the garden from different viewpoints – from inside and outside the house. Indicate which parts receive the most sun and shade and mark the direction of the prevailing wind. Highlight existing features that are to be kept, then sketch in the major structures of your new garden.

PERGOLA

This feature offers a shady corner and can be covered to provide a rainproof shelter. It also adds a third dimension to an otherwise flat space (*see p. 36*).

TREES
Apart from providing focal points, trees offer nesting places and songposts for birds. When planning the garden, take into account the shading and sheltering effects of trees, especially those near patios (*see p. 28*).

HEDGE
Useful as an informal garden boundary, a hedge makes an attractive backdrop to a flower border. It also provides good nesting sites and cover (*see p. 26*).

WILDFLOWER AREA
Ideal for growing in a site with poor soil and beneath trees, wild flowers make colourful features and will attract a variety of wildlife to the garden (*see p. 21*).

POND
Water gardens and ponds are highly valued by birds. These eye-catching features need as much planning and maintenance as any other garden feature (*see p. 44*). Banks are clever disguises for spoil left from digging a pond or builder's rubble (*see p. 38*), and are ideal for plants that prefer dry soil.

HERBACEOUS BORDER
An important part of border design is to ensure a succession of flowering for as much of the year as possible (*see pp. 32–34*).

TERRACE
A patio, courtyard, or roof garden can be enhanced by plants grown in raised beds or free-standing and hanging containers (*see p. 40*).

LAWN
An area of grass in the garden makes an ideal site for ground-feeding birds looking for insects, worms, seeds, or kitchen scraps (*see p. 20*). Ground cover at the front of beds offers seclusion for timid birds (*see p. 22*).

VEGETATION VARIETY

THE KEY TO ATTRACTING BIRDS into your garden is to offer a variety of vegetation throughout the year. A balanced mix of trees, shrubs, herbaceous perennials, and grasses will provide a range of heights and spaces to suit the feeding and nesting habits of different birds. Many garden birds look for food on lawns and in flowerbeds but they also need trees, bushes, and undergrowth in which to retreat for safety. For example, mistle thrushes hunt for worms and snails on the lawn, but also scour trees for berries. They nest in tree branches and are well known for singing stridently from their high songposts. In contrast, some birds favour just one aspect of a garden; notably, warblers and treecreepers prefer to stay in trees and are rarely seen in open spaces.

Imitating Nature
When planning a birdfeeder's garden, your aim should be to reproduce the features of the natural habitat favoured by birds. Few houses have truly natural gardens that imitate rural countryside, but many mature gardens share common features with woodland borders. This type of habitat comprises a particularly rich and varied mix of trees, shrubs, and open ground and is well suited to most garden plans. The birds most likely to visit gardens are those that divide their time between trees and open ground or live among hedgerows.

Planting for Birds
Even though there is still much to learn about the food preferences of birds, some plants should be given a priority status in your bird garden. For example, firethorn, honeysuckle, ivy, and crab apple are considered essential, while other plants are included for their horticultural interest with the hope that they are also attractive to birds visiting the garden.

The advantage of a mature garden is that it provides a longer lasting and more complete home for birds than can be achieved by simply putting out food. When setting out to create a bird garden, bear in mind that many plants, especially those that produce fruits, grow slowly. Any garden is a long-term investment that takes time to evolve as a habitat for birds. However, while the garden is still taking shape, several shortcuts, such as birdfeeders, perching posts, and "artificial" trees, can be used.

Tiered Planting
Layers of trees, shrubs, and herbaceous plants imitate the range of height and space found along woodland borders. The creation of a complex habitat offering roosts, cover, and songposts will attract birds to your garden.

A radical new way of thinking about layout and content is needed when designing a garden for birds. In particular, plants need to be selected not just for their appearance but also for their ability to provide food and shelter for birds. It is just as important to decide how much you are prepared to allow your visitors to plunder. You may welcome birds in your garden when they feed on snails, aphids, and caterpillars, but not when they strip brassicas, beans, and peas, and deplete your crop of summer fruits.

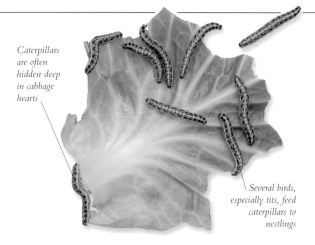

Caterpillars are often hidden deep in cabbage hearts

Several birds, especially tits, feed caterpillars to nestlings

Go for Greens
Usually grown as vegetables in kitchen gardens, cabbages and other brassicas are rarely recommended as plants to attract birds. In fact, they have more to offer than many plants in that they are good sources of caterpillars, which are common pests in vegetable plots but favourite food among hungry garden birds.

Sharing Your Crops
If you are willing to spare some of your crops, a vegetable plot is a good source of insects and larvae for hungry nestlings. Some birds are attracted to the flowers of runner beans and peas, and will feed on the tall flowerheads of brassicas that are allowed to "bolt".

LAWNS

LIKE WOODLAND CLEARINGS, lawns offer unobstructed views of the surrounding trees and shrubs in gardens. They are ideal for ground-feeding birds, which are attracted to weed seeds, insects, and scattered kitchen scraps. Closely mown lawns expose the slightest movements of worms protruding from their tunnels and are useful to feeding robins and thrushes. Starlings are often seen striding across lawns with a purposeful air. When looking for leatherjackets and other insects, they thrust their bills into the ground and squint down the holes.

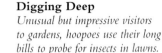

Digging Deep
Unusual but impressive visitors to gardens, hoopoes use their long bills to probe for insects in lawns.

Maintaining Your Lawn

Your main lawn can be made attractive to birds by leaving a crop of spring weeds to seed before the start of the summer mowing regime. Crops of dandelion and clover seeds will be welcomed by woodpigeons, collared doves, and finches. However, the decision to let dandelions flourish should not be taken lightly, since they spread very quickly and the leaf rosettes tend to crowd out grass. Do not remove ants' nests from your lawn since they may attract green woodpeckers, which thrust their tongues deep into the ground to lick up ants. Avoid using pesticides on your lawn. Apart from killing off an important source of food, poisons can be passed on to birds. Equally, weedkillers should be used sparingly, if at all, and targeted at weeds such as ground elder, which are difficult to dislodge and have no value to wildlife.

Watering your lawn in dry weather is a great benefit for birds because it brings earthworms to the surface. These are important for nestling blackbirds and thrushes, which may starve when dry weather drives worms deep below the surface. While not attractive to the human eye, patches of bare soil left around the edge of the lawn will be used by birds for dust-bathing.

USEFUL WEEDS

The following varieties produce good crops of seeds. Creeping buttercup spreads rapidly and brings summer colour to areas of grass. Plantain seeds are a common ingredient of bird-feed mixes. Clover flowers attract bees as well as birds and are worth keeping in all but high-quality lawns.

CREEPING BUTTERCUP
Ranunculus repens

BROAD-LEAVED PLANTAIN
Plantago major

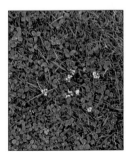

WHITE CLOVER
Trifolium repens

Creating a Wildflower Area

In a birdfeeder's garden, it is a good idea to manage at least part of your lawn as a meadow, with wild flowers growing among taller grass. This may be the best use of an area that is difficult to mow or has poor soil. For the first year, keep the grass to about 5–8 cm long. Thereafter, mow the lawn every three or four weeks once the spring flowers have seeded. Alternatively, mow occasionally through spring and then allow the summer flowers to seed. In all cases, remove the grass cuttings because wild flowers flourish better in impoverished soil. Seeds for plants such as angelica, fat hen, and goosefoot can be bought from specialist suppliers of wildflower seeds, while yarrow, thistles, and cow parsley will seed themselves.

Grass can also be allowed to grow and seed unchecked around trees and in odd corners of the garden, where nothing else grows. The rank growth will shelter many types of small animal that are hunted by predatory birds. As well as insects and snails, it might encourage mice and voles which, in turn, could draw kestrels to hover over the garden by day or tawny owls to visit at night.

Decorative Seedheads
*Ornamental grasses can be used to add height and interest to a wildflower garden or herbaceous border. The fluffy seedheads of hare's tail (*Lagurus ovatus*) attract seed-eating birds and serve as nesting material.*

Flowers in Grass
Many wild flowers are suitable for growing in meadows and provide welcome splashes of colour in large expanses of grass. When allowed to seed, they provide sources of food for birds in autumn and winter.

GROUND COVER

POPULAR AMONG "lazy gardeners" because they require little if any maintenance, ground-cover plants are ideal for filling bare patches in beds and for suppressing weeds. The essential features of ground-cover plants are that they should be dense, fast-growing perennials that persist through the winter or sprout again rapidly in spring. Although their vigorous growth crowds out weeds, ground-cover plants should not be allowed to become invasive and to smother neighbouring plants. Low-growing species can be used as substitutes for areas of lawn, such as slopes and awkward corners, which are difficult to mow. They are also useful for planting beneath trees and in areas that are difficult to cultivate.

For the birdfeeder's garden, ground cover has the additional benefit of attracting birds with its seeds, insects, and shelter. The carpet of foliage formed by St John's wort and other low-growing plants maintains a good population of insects and spiders, while dwarf junipers, cotoneasters, and heathers provide the secluded corners and overhanging foliage preferred by skulking birds, such as wrens and dunnocks.

WHAT TO PLANT
Ground-cover plants vary in size and form. The best results can be achieved by using a mix of hummock-formers, such as viburnum, grown together to form a compact bush, carpet-formers, such as comfrey and St John's wort, and spreading plants, such as nettles or cotoneasters, which tend to be vigorous.

HONEYSUCKLE
Birds often roost in the evergreen foliage of honeysuckle (see p. 104).

OREGON GRAPE
The fragrant flowers of Oregon grape attract birds that feed on the nectar and pollen (see p. 104).

VIBURNUM
Insect-eating birds enjoy the aphids and whitefly often found on viburnum leaves (see p. 105).

COTONEASTER MICROPHYLLUS
The brightly coloured fruits of cotoneaster are enjoyed by garden birds (see p. 102).

Taking Cover
Dunnocks are shy, skulking birds that tend to keep to the cover of hedges and shrubs when looking for insects and seeds.

SPOTTED DEADNETTLE
Lamium maculata
This is a semi-evergreen plant whose white or mauve flowers are pollinated by bumblebees. The nutlets are eaten by finches.

WILD CHERRY
*The crop of red fruits on this small,
deciduous tree is quickly stripped
by garden birds* (see p. 114).

COMFREY
Symphytum spp.
This carpet plant bears drooping,
tubular flowers in shades of blue,
pink, or white. It grows well in
shady borders or under trees.

COTONEASTER
HORIZONTALIS
*The compact foliage of
cotoneaster provides good
cover for birds* (see p. 102).

IVY
*Ivy berries are a valuable
source of winter food for
birds* (see p. 103).

WILD STRAWBERRY
*Strawberries are a favourite
food of many garden birds*
(see p. 107).

ST JOHN'S WORT
*The yellow flowers of this dense,
evergreen carpet-former are
pollinated by insects* (see p. 111).

SHRUBS

THE DISTINCTION BETWEEN shrubs and trees is not always clear. Both are perennials with woody stems but, typically, a shrub's branches spring from the base of the plant while a tree has a single trunk with branches at some distance above the ground. Shrubs play an important role in the design of a garden. Even in winter, a mixture of evergreen and deciduous shrubs will provide interest with their colour and form. For example, hazel and dogwood have attractive stems, while mahonia and viburnum produce winter flowers. A large choice of shrubs is available, covering every horticultural requirement and providing plenty of possibilities for the birdfeeder's garden.

SKIMMIA JAPONICA 'RUBELLA'   *SENECIO MARITIMA*   *SOLANUM CAPSICASTRUM*

Winter Colour
Small shrubs suit windowboxes and patio tubs. They can be planted up to provide year-round colour, using varieties whose flowers and seeds will attract birds.

Using Colour and Form

As well as choosing varieties that suit your garden's environment, in terms of exposure, soil, and drainage, take care to select the most suitable sizes and positions. When planning a layout, you might find it useful to place canes in the ground at the expected height and position of each shrub. This helps to judge the overall effect of a planting scheme when it has matured. Consider the range of colours that you will be using in your planting scheme to

Specimen Shrub
*The well-defined structure of the Japanese snowball bush (*Viburnum plicatum)* makes a strong focal point in the garden. Its cloak of white flowers matures to red-purple in autumn. Some* Viburnum *species produce autumn berries (see p. 105); although the snowball bush does not fruit, birds are attracted to the large number of aphids that thrive on the leaves during summer.*

ensure balance and seasonal interest. A large garden can host a selection of shrubs to provide a succession of colour, whereas smaller gardens are better suited to shrubs with long flowering periods, such as the lilac *Syringa microphylla* 'Superba', which flowers from spring through to autumn.

Large shrubs are useful for dividing a garden into sections or screening off unsightly areas. You can also use them to soften hard angles on buildings or, when planted at the rear of a border, to provide a backdrop for a display of colourful, summer flowers. Plant small shrubs on patios and roof gardens or in windowboxes, and choose wall shrubs for small gardens to make the most of limited space. The warmth and shelter of a wall are suitable for tender shrubs that survive in the open, but make sure that these plants receive plenty of water. One added advantage of planting shrubs is that routine care involves little more than trimming, weeding, and mulching. Plant any new shrubs in the autumn, when the soil is still warm. This enables the

Secure Site
A gorse bush provides a good site for nesting long-tailed tits. The spiny growth offers protection from predators.

roots to become established before the leaves start to grow in spring. Shrubs may also be transplanted to a new site in autumn if your garden needs to be reorganized or renovated, when a new feature is to be added, or if you have made a mistake in your original garden plan.

Providing Winter Rations

For birds, shrubs such as barberry and firethorn provide good cover, especially when they have dense growths of twigs and foliage. Birds are most attracted by shrubs that yield crops of fruits and seeds, although a bed of shrubs also makes a large surface area that attracts insects, snails, and other small animals. Despite most fruits and seeds being ripe by late summer, they often remain uneaten far into winter. Once other sources of food are exhausted, you will notice that these fruits suddenly disappear as birds descend on them to feed.

PLANTING A WALL SHRUB

1 *Dig a hole about 30 cm away from the wall. Plant the shrub (here, Pyracantha) and tie its supporting cane to the wire or trellis on which it will grow.*

2 *Using twine, tie horizontal canes to the central cane and wires to support and train the sideshoots. Make sure that these shoots will not be damaged by any wind movement.*

HEDGES

IN THE COUNTRYSIDE, hedgerows provide many birds with food and shelter. Whether informal or clipped, hedges can play a similar role in your bird garden. When grown to more than 1.5 m high and 1 m thick, they will provide ideal nesting sites as well as effective cover from predators. Small birds can dive deep into hedges to escape the reach of a sparrowhawk's talons, and cats are soon deterred from pursuing a bird when confronted by a thicket of twigs, especially thorny foliage.

Well-hidden Nest
Bullfinches build their delicate nests among dense twigs, often in evergreen plants such as privet.

Rows of densely planted shrubs can be used to form a screen or informal boundary marker. Many hedges are solid blocks of a single species, such as privet or beech. Both visually and for birds, hedging is enhanced when a variety of species is used. Blackthorn, holly, hawthorn, and elder are the most popular hedges with birds, but keep elder in check because it is vigorous and quickly grows out of control. The best hedges are produced by hard pruning in the first two years to encourage a dense branch structure. If possible, trim

Informal Hedge
Flowering quince (Chaenomeles japonica) *is a deciduous, shiny shrub that is good as informal, low hedging. Its clusters of scarlet flowers are followed by yellow fruits in autumn.*

USEFUL PLANTS FOR HEDGING	
SPECIES	HEIGHT
Deciduous	
Beech	1–6 m
Blackthorn	2–4 m
Hawthorn	2–3 m
Hazel	2–5 m
Hornbeam	1.5–6 m
Evergreen	
Barberry (some)	1.5–2 m
Firethorn	2–3 m
Holly	1.5–2 m
Honeysuckle	1–1.5 m
Lavender	0.5–1 m
Leyland cypress	2–6 m
Privet	1–3 m
Japanese spindle	1–3 m
Yew	1–6 m

Hedging Varieties
Each of these shrubs is suitable for hedging in gardens. By mixing several species, the flowering and fruiting season can be extended to provide a reliable nesting site and source of food for birds through most of the year.

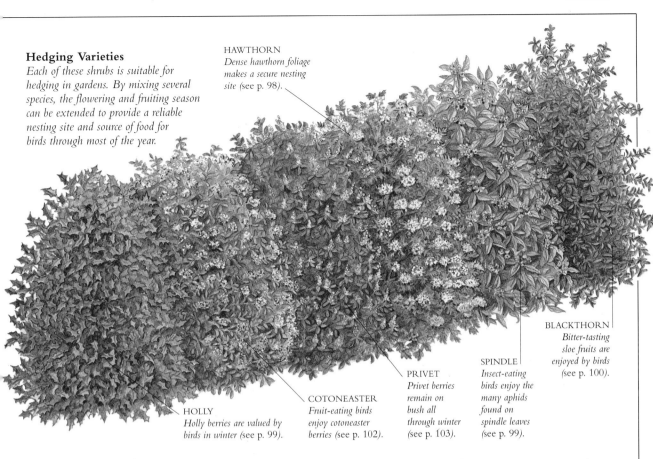

HAWTHORN
Dense hawthorn foliage makes a secure nesting site (see p. 98).

BLACKTHORN
Bitter-tasting sloe fruits are enjoyed by birds (see p. 100).

SPINDLE
Insect-eating birds enjoy the many aphids found on spindle leaves (see p. 99).

PRIVET
Privet berries remain on bush all through winter (see p. 103).

COTONEASTER
Fruit-eating birds enjoy cotoneaster berries (see p. 102).

HOLLY
Holly berries are valued by birds in winter (see p. 99).

sections of hedge in alternate years to allow flowering. The best time for trimming is late winter or early spring, after the berries have been eaten and before birds are nesting. Privet is usually clipped hard for a formal hedge, but if allowed to become slightly untidy it produces tiny flowers and black berries. Hawthorn flowers and fruits only on overwintered stems. Leyland cypress is frequently planted to make a quick-growing screen, but make sure that the top of the hedge can be reached easily with a ladder and long-handled secateurs for pruning. Brighten up large blocks of dark green foliage and give your hedge added wildlife interest by intertwining honeysuckle or climbing roses.

Planting a hedge follows the same rules as for trees and shrubs (*see p. 53*). Weed and rake the ground in a strip of up to 1 m wide and lay a marker line so that the hedge is planted true and straight. Most hedging plants are spaced at intervals of 30 cm to 45 cm, or 60 cm for vigorous plants. Wide, dense hedges can be achieved by planting in double, staggered rows.

Sheltering Exposed Plants

Gardens on exposed hillsides and coastal sites, or those subject to wind funnels between buildings need shelter. Windbreaks protect plants from snapped limbs and prevent them from blowing over. They also shield against desiccation, which "scorches" the growing tips of stems, and may be used by birds for shelter on cold nights. Hedges shield more effectively than walls or solid fences because they allow wind to pass through, but at a reduced speed and without turbulence. In contrast, solid windbreaks merely deflect the wind upwards, allowing turbulence to form behind them.

TREES

ALTHOUGH FEW GARDENS are large enough to accommodate many trees, it should be possible to include at least one or two of the smaller species. Trees add a third dimension to a garden and are often used to make strong focal points. Planted in small groups, they can be trained to form screens, arches, or boundary dividers. In the bird garden, trees create extra habitat with nesting places and songposts, and supply a variety of food. When several are planted close to each other, they form a continuous canopy that is much-favoured by warblers. Deciduous forest trees, such as oak, are an important source of caterpillars, which are the main food for nestling tits. Some trees, however, have negative aspects. For example, the dense, evergreen foliage of yews prevents underplanting, lime trees drip honeydew, and the surface roots of *Prunus* species throw up suckers and make cultivation

Choosing a Tree
Trees can be bought with bare roots, root-balled, or container-grown. A healthy specimen should have evenly spread roots, and a well-developed, balanced shape around the stem. Check for disease and damage before purchase.

Central leader

Healthy-looking foliage

Well-balanced shape

Firm root-ball

FOOD FROM TREES

Blossoms
While flowers are not very nutritious, they are plentiful in spring when other sources of food for birds are often scarce.

Catkins
These "tails" of seeds are welcomed by birds because they appear at the end of winter when food supplies are running low.

Fruits
Many garden birds are attracted to the juicy flesh of garden fruits such as pears (see p. 110), while some birds eat only the seeds.

difficult. It is best to plant large, vigorous trees, including willows and poplars, away from walls and buildings because their roots can cause damage to foundations.

Trees are planted as long-term investments. Unless you already have a mature garden, you must be prepared to wait at least five years for your saplings to take shape. For quicker returns, choose fast-growing species like evergreen Leyland cypresses or deciduous willows and poplars, which may grow by 1 m or more a year and will need to be kept under control. Alternatively, you can select smaller trees such as a weeping Kilmarnock willow, which grows only 2 m high (*see p. 101*), an ornamental bird cherry (*see p. 114*), or rowan (*see p. 115*), which is tolerant of atmospheric pollution.

Conspicuous Perch
Mistle thrushes often sing their loud, ringing song from high perches, such as the tops of spruce trees.

Coppicing and Pollarding
Hazel, willow, sweet chestnut, and poplar suit coppicing and pollarding. These two methods of tree and shrub management can be used in gardens to control growth. They are best carried out in late winter or early spring. Coppicing involves cutting the trunk of a tree to form a "stool" near the ground, with the stems cut close to the stool and at an angle so that rainwater runs away from the trunk. In the following season, new shoots spring rapidly from the stool to form a bushy growth. Pollarded trees are cut at head height to create well-shaped "bushy-topped" trees.

Underplanting
Provided that the foliage is not too dense and low, an attractive variety of woodland and shade-loving plants can be grown under trees.

Specimen Tree
The fast-growing Robinia pseudoacacia *'Frisia' is suitable for small gardens. Its airy, lime-green foliage makes a splash of bright colour.*

CLIMBERS

PLANTS that attach themselves to supports are collectively known as climbers. They offer a simple and effective way of bringing variety into gardens and are popular with birds. Useful for covering and softening bare walls or enlivening formal hedges, climbers bring colour and scent to dull corners. They also offer a quick solution for adding height and are especially valuable in small gardens and courtyards because they occupy very little ground space.

Most climbers provide cover for roosting and nesting in the bird garden, but honeysuckle and ivy are particularly valuable plants. Their fruits are popular with birds and their dense growth provides excellent shelter. Ivy has a special

Sweet Berries
Robins are mainly insect eaters, but they enjoy feeding on berries such as honeysuckle in autumn.

importance because it flowers in autumn and produces berries in winter when food is scarce. Clematis is suitable for cloaking unsightly structures, and its buds are eaten by bullfinches. Perhaps more so for climbers than other plants, it is necessary to consult plant catalogues and gardening books before choosing climbers. Select a plant that suits the height and area to be covered, and the type of support. Some species, such as Virginia creeper, are very vigorous, so make sure that you have access for trimming the plant.

TYPES OF CLIMBER

The methods used by climbing plants to scramble towards light can be divided into four groups: aerial, leaf-stalk, tendril, and twining. The climbing method of a plant determines which type of natural or purpose-built support will be the most appropriate. Self-clinging climbers only need to be supported until they have established secure contact, while twining species need permanent support.

Aerial Roots
(Ivy)
Some self-clinging climbers attach to any surface, using tiny, aerial rootlets borne on the stem.

Leaf Stalks
(Clematis)
These climbers gain height and spread by means of leaf stalks wrapping themselves around supports.

Tendrils
(Passion flower)
Adhesive tendril tips, often modified leaves or side shoots, can attach themselves to any surface.

Twining Stems
(Chocolate vine)
Twining climbers coil around any nearby support, in either a counter- or clockwise direction.

Adding Interest

Climbers are useful for brightening up blocks of dull foliage, such as screens of Leyland cypress or yew. Choose honeysuckle, *Clematis montana*, Virginia creeper, or rambling roses, all of which readily climb through shrubs and trees. For a range of flower colours, combine climbers of similar habit. Make sure that the expected growths of the climber and support plant are compatible so that the host plant is not swamped by an over-vigorous climber. An old trunk or tree stump can be transformed into a focal point, when trailing or scrambling climbers are allowed to cascade over or sprawl across the base and any remaining branches. Grape vine, honeysuckle, and wisteria can all be grown as standards. They suit patios and walkways, and can be used as "artificial trees"

Clambering Through Climbers
In winter, woodpigeons can be seen clambering over the dense growth of ivy in search of berries.

Providing Routine Care

Plant climbers at 30–50 cm from a supporting wall or evergreen tree or shrub to ensure that they are not in a "rain shadow" and receive enough water at the roots. Whether planting near a wall or under a tree, feed and water the plants regularly since the soil is likely to be poor and dry. Tie the main stems to the supports and cut back sideshoots to 15–30 cm. As a climber grows, guide twining stems and tendrils to cling to the supports and train the main shoots while they are still young and pliable, to spread over the area to be covered. When training a climber as a standard, provide a permanent stake or frame to support the trunk of the plant.

Cutting Back Climbers
To obtain a natural effect when cutting back climbers that have sprawled beyond their allotted area, trim back the stems irregularly with secateurs.

Well-cloaked Wall
*A vigorous, fast-growing plant, climbing hydrangea (*Hydrangea petiolaris*) can be trained to form an attractive backdrop.*

SPRING HERBACEOUS BORDER

AFTER THE DRABNESS OF WINTER, spring bulbs, such as crocus, daffodil, and grape hyacinth, brighten up the garden. The mass of colour produced by the flowers attracts insects which, in turn, attract birds. However, the reasons why some birds are drawn to flowers are less clear. For example, house sparrows frustrate gardeners when they strip petals from crocuses and primulas for no special purpose. Crown imperials make an interesting addition to borders because they are visited by blue tits, blackcaps, and garden warblers, which sip the nectar and help to pollinate the flowers. When the seeds of primroses, winter aconites, and winter-flowering violets ripen in spring they are welcomed by birds, since winter seedstocks have usually been exhausted. Likewise, early-flowering dandelions and groundsel are enjoyed by bullfinches and goldfinches.

Herbaceous beds provide nesting material, too. Starlings' nests are sometimes lined with the leaves of yarrow, agrimony, and fleabane, whose insecticidal properties kill parasites.

Sipping Nectar
Blackcaps are attracted by the nectar of crown imperials, which supplements their diets in spring.

FORSYTHIA
Forsythia spp.
The yellow flowers of forsythia bring colour to the garden in early spring and are important for insects. The dense growth is used by nesting birds.

WISTERIA
Wisteria spp.
This twining climber bears fragrant flowers in spring, followed by long, thin seedpods in summer.

Gathering Nesting Material
Song thrushes can be seen gathering nest material, such as dead leaves, rootlets, and grasses, among flowering bulbs.

WHAT TO PLANT

Select flowering bulbs that produce a succession of colour throughout spring. Intersperse them with ornamental grasses for height and interest in the flowerbed. Backdrops of wisteria and forsythia trained on panels of trellis provide useful roosting sites for birds.

GOLDEN OATS

Stipia spp.
Birds use this decorative grass for weaving into delicate cup-nests.

SILVER BIRCH
The winged seeds and yellow catkins of silver birch are enjoyed by birds (see p. 114).

BUGLE
Ajuga reptans
This low-growing plant forms a mat of semi-evergreen foliage and bears blue flowers. It grows well under shrubs and prefers damp soil.

CROCUS
The colourful petals of these goblet-shaped flowers often attract birds in spring (see p. 127).

PRIMROSE
Birds feed on aphids found on the colourful primrose flowers (see p. 111).

VIOLET
Good for a woodland garden, violets bear seeds in autumn (see p. 111).

DAISY
Bellis perennis
Daisies are considered to be a weed on lawns, but cultivated varieties are grown in borders for their flowers. When left to seed, they are enjoyed by garden birds.

CROWN IMPERIAL
This spring bulb produces a head of bell-shaped flowers on a tall stem (see p. 127).

FORGET-ME-NOT
Birds are attracted to the slugs and snails that feed on forget-me-nots (see p. 107).

Autumn Herbaceous Border

With careful planting, a well-tended, autumn herbaceous border can provide a vivid display of colour and attract a range of birds feeding on insects, nectar, and seeds.

Traditionally, herbaceous beds require a considerable amount of attention to keep them in good order, but the trend towards low-maintenance gardens has changed attitudes towards their upkeep. Instead of rigorously cutting back the summer's growth after flowering, you can often retain dead stems and foliage as features in their own right, valued for their colours and shapes. If dead stems are cut to the ground as soon as flowering finishes and before seeds and fruit have set, they lose their value in the bird garden. Taller stems, especially those bearing large flowerheads, may benefit from staking. Keep the soil in a bed clear of weeds and protect it from droughts and frost by applying a protective layer of mulch before the onset of winter.

What to Plant
Choose perennials that give good ground cover and require little management in the border. The flowering season of some summer-flowering plants can be extended into autumn by deadheading the first crop of flowers. The seeds of the second crop then become a useful food resource for birds through winter.

Ornamental Onion
Allium spp.
These decorative varieties of onion are planted as bulbs. Some flower in late summer and autumn, and their dense flowers ripen into seedheads that are attractive to birds.

Barberry
Barberry's colourful berries attract birds in late summer and autumn (see p. 123).

Sunflower
Birds are attracted to the tightly packed seedheads of ripe sunflowers (see p. 125).

Woolly Thistle
Cirsium eriophorum
Thistles are very popular with goldfinches, which tear up the heads to reach the seeds.

Foxglove
Digitalis purpurea
Tall spikes of foxgloves bear showy flowers, which are visited by bumblebees throughout the summer. Scattered seeds will be found by birds foraging in the bed.

Welted Thistle
The tall, purple flowerheads attract insects (see p. 106).

St John's Wort
Finches love the autumn fruits of this dense, evergreen carpet-former (see p. 111).

Michaelmas Daisy
Finches enjoy the seedheads that follow the autumn clusters of purple flowers (see p. 111).

Clearing Litter
A heap of crab-apple leaves and honesty seedpods provides an ideal hiding place for insects and other small animals. Blackbirds flick through leaf litter with their bills and scrape it with their feet in search of morsels to eat.

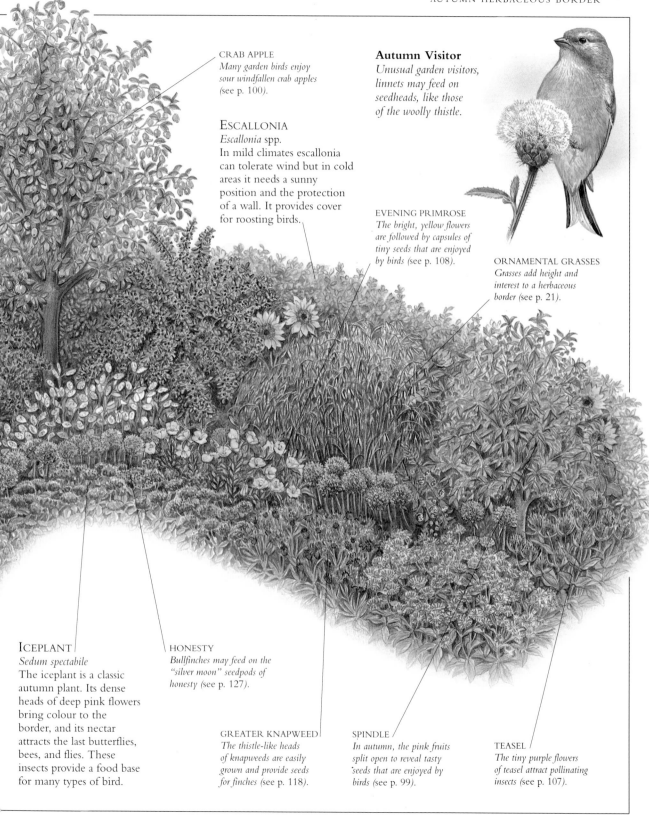

CRAB APPLE
*Many garden birds enjoy
sour windfallen crab apples
(see p. 100).*

Autumn Visitor
*Unusual garden visitors,
linnets may feed on
seedheads, like those
of the woolly thistle.*

ESCALLONIA
Escallonia spp.
In mild climates escallonia
can tolerate wind but in cold
areas it needs a sunny
position and the protection
of a wall. It provides cover
for roosting birds.

EVENING PRIMROSE
*The bright, yellow flowers
are followed by capsules of
tiny seeds that are enjoyed
by birds (see p. 108).*

ORNAMENTAL GRASSES
*Grasses add height and
interest to a herbaceous
border (see p. 21).*

ICEPLANT
Sedum spectabile
The iceplant is a classic
autumn plant. Its dense
heads of deep pink flowers
bring colour to the
border, and its nectar
attracts the last butterflies,
bees, and flies. These
insects provide a food base
for many types of bird.

HONESTY
*Bullfinches may feed on the
"silver moon" seedpods of
honesty (see p. 127).*

GREATER KNAPWEED
*The thistle-like heads
of knapweeds are easily
grown and provide seeds
for finches (see p. 118).*

SPINDLE
*In autumn, the pink fruits
split open to reveal tasty
seeds that are enjoyed by
birds (see p. 99).*

TEASEL
*The tiny purple flowers
of teasel attract pollinating
insects (see p. 107).*

PERGOLAS AND TRELLISES

OFTEN OVERLOOKED in garden design, pergolas and trellises can make valuable contributions to the birdfeeder's garden. The term "pergola" used to refer to paths lined by trellises covered in climbing plants, but now it includes open frameworks of timber uprights and beams over which plants grow. Where a site is too small or unsuitable for growing trees, pergolas and trellises offer practical alternatives for adding height and interest to a garden. They can also be used as supports for climbers, or as frameworks for training fruit trees.

A lawn or a herbaceous border is improved by a feature that gives it height and forms a focal point. While the natural answer is a tree, the quicker solution is a trellis pillar, which birds will accept as a tree and use for perching, nesting, and feeding. Pillars can be custom-built or made from four ready-made trellis panels fastened together and attached to metal post supports. Train a selection of climbers over the pillar to provide foliage and fruit for the "artificial tree", and add a nestbox or feeder hanging from a bracket to attract birds.

Trellis Pillar
A pillar or "wigwam" of trellis can serve as an artificial tree. It is especially useful in new gardens, where the trees and shrubs have yet to mature.

Traditional Pergola
Fruit trees such as Prunus, trained over a series of arches along a garden path, make an attractive focal point.

Making Pergolas

Rustic pergolas are often made from wooden poles, sometimes with the bark still attached, but it is more usual to use sawn timber. When calculating how much wood is needed, allow enough width and height for an arch, because plants quickly reduce the space once they are established. Make sure that the wood chosen is sound. It is best to soak any sawn ends in a can of non-toxic preservative for 24 hours, even though it should already be impregnated with preservative – time spent in preservation will be rewarded with longer lasting timber. Wood rot is most common at or below ground level, but can be eliminated by standing posts in free-draining gravel, supports, or square brick shoes on a concrete foundation.

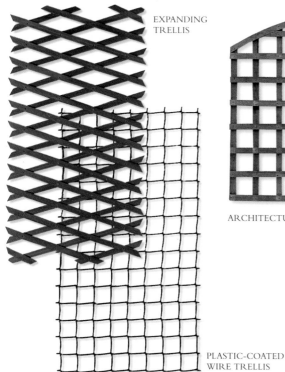

Lookout Post

A nestbox hidden among the foliage on a trellis pillar provides a good vantage point for its resident great tit.

Choosing Trellises

When selecting from the variety of trellises available, opt for a strong one since it may eventually carry a considerable weight of vegetation, and make sure that it is firmly fixed to the support. Trellises are useful for blocking in sections of a pergola, screening unsightly objects, and extending the height of a fence. If the trellis is to be attached to a wall, allow a gap of at least 5 cm so that air can circulate behind the plants. Attach vertical battens to the wall with masonry nails, screws, or wall bolts, then fix the trellis to the battens so that it can be taken down easily for routine maintenance.

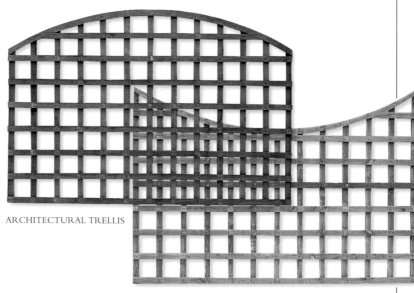

EXPANDING TRELLIS

ARCHITECTURAL TRELLIS

PLASTIC-COATED WIRE TRELLIS

Types of Trellis

Several patterns of trellis and other types of frame can be bought for training climbing plants. Some are shaped to provide architectural features in a garden. Plastic-coated wire is less expensive and easier to erect than rigid frames. Expanding trellis can be adjusted to the required size.

WALLS AND BANKS

A HIGH BOUNDARY WALL is the most effective and permanent type of screen, although it can be the most expensive and difficult to erect. A bare wall draped with a range of trellis-grown climbers and wall shrubs, and decorated with smaller plants, can play a useful role in a birdfeeder's garden.

For safety, it is best to gain professional advice for the construction of any wall that exceeds 1 m high. Essentially, all walls must have proper foundations or footing that is twice the width of the wall and 40 cm deep. Allow a series of gaps or "weep holes" in the lower course of a brick wall to permit drainage,

and edge the top of the wall with coping stones. These give a "finish" to the top of the wall and keep out rain water, which can seep into joints and damage the brickwork.

If space allows, build a double, free-standing brick wall so that it has a cavity, as in the walls of a house. Leave weep holes along the bottom and other gaps higher up the wall. Fill the bottom of the cavity with rubble, top up with soil, and insert plants in the gaps. A fringe of plants can be grown along the top of the wall. A stone wall, made with blocks of natural stone and strengthened with mortar, is an attractive alternative to bricks. For a dry-stone wall,

PLANTING A WALL MANGER

1 Line the base and sides of the manger with 1–2 cm of moss, and firm down well. Add a thin layer of multi-purpose compost.

2 Position trailing plants from inside the manger, teasing them so that they hang easily through the sides. Firm gently into the compost.

3 Build up the manger with more moss lining and compost, then add another layer of plants. Repeat this method until the manger is full.

Completed Wall Manger

Wall and hanging baskets can brighten up a large expanse of bare wall and are an effective use of space in small gardens and courtyards. As well as being attracted by the insects that pollinate the flowers, birds may even nest in a well-planted wall manger.

EUONYMUS FORTUNEI 'EMERALD GAIETY'

CYCLAMEN CILICIUM

AJUGA REPTANS 'BRAUNHERZ'

LAMIUM MACULATUM 'WHITE NANCY'

plants can be inserted directly into soil between the courses, but gaps can be left during construction to take larger plants, such as thrift, wallflowers, aubretia, and alyssum. It is a good idea to leave some recesses empty since they may be used as nesting places by robins, wrens, or wagtails.

Hole in the Wall
A wren may make its nest in a purpose-made recess in a wall covered with dense creepers.

Raised Beds and Banks

Retaining walls can be used to break a slope into terraces and banks. These create visual interest in a garden and are easy to manage. Raised beds are useful in small gardens or courtyards where space is restricted. Being fully adaptable in height and size, they can be purpose-built to make gardening possible for those with limited mobility. Filled with a specific type of soil, raised beds can accommodate plants with special cultural needs, such as acid-loving heathers. You can also create a rock garden in a raised bed or grow herbs for culinary use. Many of these plants will bear seeds that attract birds.

Planting in a Dry Stone Wall
Carefully insert small plants or seedlings into the gaps with the aid of a knife. Press in compost to hold the plants in place. Keep the compost moist and well firmed until the plants are established.

A Well-furnished Rock Garden
A sloping rock garden allows a variety of plants to be displayed to best effect. For birds, the interest is the food that they can find among the nooks and crannies of the stonework and under the low-growing plants.

TERRACES

Hard-surfaced patios, roof gardens, and courtyards are low-maintenance areas, usually decorated with pergolas, trellises, raised beds, and containers. A patio often serves as a link between a house and its garden, and is a useful place from where visiting birds can be observed easily. While space is too restricted for plants to grow in loose profusion, you can still attract birds by using simple but effective devices, such as feeders, birdtables, and birdbaths. The most common garden birds will soon be drawn to your patio, although more timid species that prefer cover are unlikely to be seen.

WHAT TO PLANT
Given the limited space, patios and roof gardens usually adopt a formal layout. Pergolas, baskets, and patio tubs give structure to the design and increase the space available for planting.

SILVER BIRCH
When mature, silver birch trunks provide ideal nesting holes for birds (see p. 114).

GRAPE VINE
Juicy grapes are a favourite food of birds (see p. 124).

CLEMATIS
Clematis spp.
Early-flowering clematis, such as *C. montana*, are evergreen and need warm, south-facing walls.

BUBBLE FOUNTAIN
Birds enjoy washing and drinking in running water (see p. 43).

SKIMMIA
Skimmia spp.
Male and female skimmia plants are needed to produce the round, scarlet berries in late spring and early summer.

Using Containers

Terracotta pots, old sinks, and troughs can be used for summer planting. Try to position containers while they are still empty, choosing sheltered sites that receive sun for at least some of the day. Part-fill each container with broken pottery, coarse gravel, or stones as drainage and top up with moist potting compost. Hanging baskets, suspended from a pergola or pillar, may be used

Vantage Point

A spotted flycatcher nests in a hanging basket lined with toadflax, and surveys its surroundings.

by birds as nesting sites or roosts. Use a mix of flowering and trailing plants to maintain a display of all-round foliage in each basket. Always keep it well watered to prevent the moss lining from drying out, and sprinkle regularly with fertilizer to replace any nutrients that may have been washed out.

BIRDTABLE
Visiting birds can be watched at close quarters on a patio (see p. 82).

LAVENDER
Lavender flowers attract bees and other beneficial insects (see p. 123).

STRAWBERRY
Birds enjoy the seed-coated flesh of strawberries (see p. 107).

PLANTING LIST

From top to bottom

HERB BED
Mint, marjoram, purple basil, tricolour sage, creeping rosemary, parsley, feverfew, thyme

BAY TREE
Plants grown as standards serve as artificial trees (see p. 31).

CREEPING JENNY
Lysimachia nummularia 'Aurea'
This creeping perennial has round, lime-green leaves, and bears bright yellow flowers in summer.

HEARTSEASE
A member of the viola family, wild pansies flower most of the year and spread rapidly by self-sowing (see p. 111).

HERBS
A herb bed near the kitchen is a practical feature in any garden. Some herbs, such as marjoram, provide seeds for birds.

BIRDS AND WATER

WATER IS IMPORTANT to birds for drinking and bathing and, sometimes, to help them feed. Crows will use water to soften hard food, such as breadcrusts, before eating it. Few water birds hunt in gardens, although herons will sometimes visit small garden ponds to steal fish or frogs, and even blackbirds and wrens have been known to seize small water animals.

Remember to provide a supply of water in warm weather, when birds have to replace fluid they have lost to keep cool. In winter, they drink more when they are feeding on dry seeds rather than on juicy insects or fruits. A source of water in the garden is essential in sub-zero weather, when natural supplies are frozen.

Bathing in water is enjoyed by birds throughout the year. The main function is not to clean the plumage but to dampen the feathers so that they are easier to preen. This routine is just as important in cold weather because it helps to maintain the insulating properties of the plumage. There are various ways of providing water for garden birds, from simple water bowls to fountains and ponds.

Using Birdbaths

A variety of birdbaths is available from garden centres but a home-made version is equally good, and can be devised using a dustbin lid, flowerpot base, or large dish. Always check that the birdbath is suitable from a bird's point of view. It should have sloping sides that allow small birds to bathe at the edges, and must have a central depth of about 9 cm to enable large birds to soak themselves. It should also hold sufficient water to withstand a vigorous bathing session by a flock of starlings, which can often empty a birdbath in just one visit.

The position of a birdbath in your garden is critical, because birds will not use it unless they feel safe. Since wet plumage makes it harder for them to take flight from danger, birds need the bath to be sited close to a bush or cover where they can take refuge to dry and preen. Try placing the birdbath at different points around the garden to find the most popular site. In winter, thaw the birdbath with boiling water or, in prolonged periods of frost, float a rubber ball on the surface of the water. This forms an

MAKING A SIMPLE BIRDBATH

1 Bend a hardboard strip into a circle, nailing the ends to a wooden block. Pour a mortar mix into the mould, shaping the mix into a shallow dish.

2 Once the dish has set hard, smooth it with a metal plate, then remove the mould. Firmly fix the bath to a plinth or pedestal, or place it on the ground.

Preparing a Barrel
A half-barrel lends itself to use as a miniature pond. Coat the inside with aquaseal or bitumen, and leave to dry before use.

Remove any rotten or loose material before use

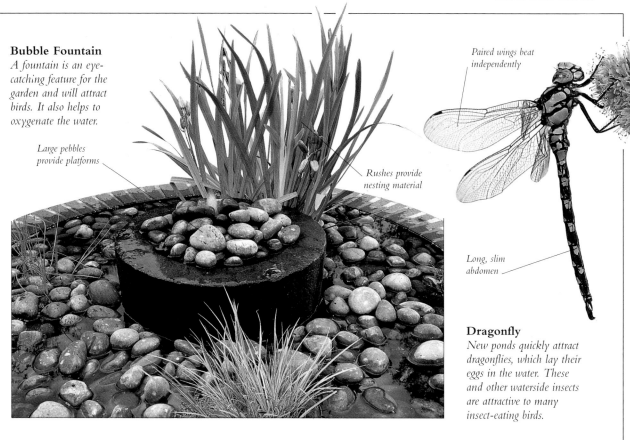

Bubble Fountain
A fountain is an eye-catching feature for the garden and will attract birds. It also helps to oxygenate the water.

Large pebbles provide platforms

Rushes provide nesting material

Paired wings beat independently

Long, slim abdomen

Dragonfly
New ponds quickly attract dragonflies, which lay their eggs in the water. These and other waterside insects are attractive to many insect-eating birds.

access hole in the ice when water freezes over. Alternatively, install an aquarium heater and thermostat. Antifreeze or salt must never be used as they are harmful to wildlife.

Providing Fountains and Sprays

Running water makes an attractive focal point in the garden and will be visited regularly by birds. It can be as simple or as decorative as you like, from a water spout to a highly ornamental fountain or meandering watercourse (*see p. 46*). You may already have a natural source in your garden such as a running stream. If space is too restricted for a pond, or if you have young children who have yet to learn the dangers of water, one practical solution is to build a bubble or cobble fountain. The base for this can either be a small, shallow patch of ground, lined with cement, or a ready-made container such as

a trough or millstone, covered in large pebbles. Using a small, submersible pump, water can be "bubbled" over the stones into a small underground reservoir. Although some marginal plants dislike growing in disturbed water, reedmace and sedges planted in the fountain will add height and interest. They will also attract aquatic flies and beetles, on which birds may feed. If the site is not suitable for planting, then make a border around the fountain with container-grown plants, such as heartsease, primulas, ferns, and trailing ivies.

In summer, many birds lose fluid trying to keep cool and actively seek out running water. A garden sprinkler or hose placed on the lawn to spray the surrounding grass and plants will soon attract a gathering of birds, eager to refresh themselves. However, local watering restrictions may limit this practice during prolonged dry spells or water shortages.

PONDS AND WATER GARDENS

WHILE PONDS OR WATER GARDENS are not essential items in a birdfeeder's garden, they are attractive to birds for drinking and bathing. If a bog garden is established alongside, wagtails and other garden birds will come to forage for worms and insects, and blackbirds, thrushes, and house martins will use the mud for nesting material.

Large ponds will attract water birds, such as ducks and herons. Moorhens feed mainly on land but need a pond of 20–40 sq m for nesting, while mallards often nest at some

distance from water. Coots and grebes require large expanses of water, beyond the scope of the average garden, but kingfishers have been known to call on garden ponds.

The best time to plant up a pond is late spring when the water is beginning to warm up. Submerge the plants in plastic baskets or flower pots and, if necessary, weight the pots with stones until the trapped air has dispersed. Place the containers on large stones or bricks so that the leaves are at surface level. The plants can gradually be lowered as the leaves spread

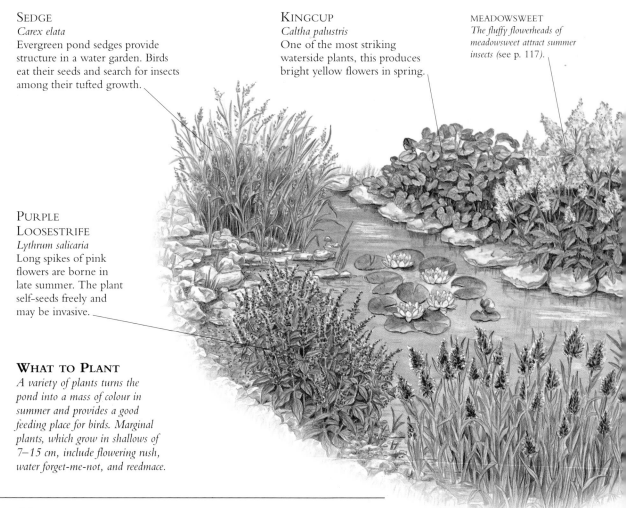

SEDGE
Carex elata
Evergreen pond sedges provide structure in a water garden. Birds eat their seeds and search for insects among their tufted growth.

KINGCUP
Caltha palustris
One of the most striking waterside plants, this produces bright yellow flowers in spring.

MEADOWSWEET
The fluffy flowerheads of meadowsweet attract summer insects (see p. 117).

PURPLE LOOSESTRIFE
Lythrum salicaria
Long spikes of pink flowers are borne in late summer. The plant self-seeds freely and may be invasive.

WHAT TO PLANT
A variety of plants turns the pond into a mass of colour in summer and provides a good feeding place for birds. Marginal plants, which grow in shallows of 7–15 cm, include flowering rush, water forget-me-not, and reedmace.

out. Lift the plants regularly for trimming and repotting. Only one or two plants are needed for a small pond, so seek advice from your local plant centre on the most suitable varieties to grow. Pondweed, which has submerged or floating leaves, adds interest to the surface of the water, while marginals such as sedges, purple loosestrife, and kingcups provide colour and variety around the edge of a pond.

Introducing Wildlife

Populations of small water creatures can be started by adding a bucket of water from an established pond. Frogs and toads can be introduced as spawn in spring, while water

beetles, dragonflies, and water boatmen will find their own way to the pond. Goldfish or sticklebacks can be valuable additions, although goldfish tend to stir up sediment. A pond takes some time to establish itself, and you may find that visitors such as water fleas or water striders appear in swarms and then disappear again.

Taking Safety Precautions

Filling in a pond for the safety of young children denies them the fun of a pond when they are older. Instead, use fencing or cover the pond with weldmesh. If your pond is small, fill it with large pebbles to reduce the water depth, or adapt it to a bubble fountain (see p. 43).

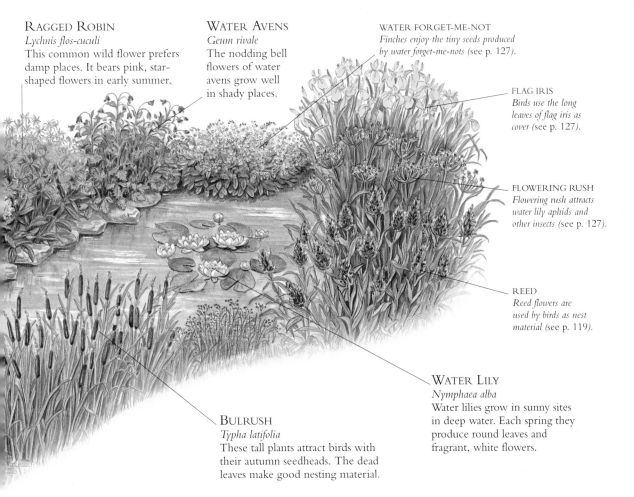

RAGGED ROBIN
Lychnis flos-cuculi
This common wild flower prefers damp places. It bears pink, star-shaped flowers in early summer.

WATER AVENS
Geum rivale
The nodding bell flowers of water avens grow well in shady places.

WATER FORGET-ME-NOT
Finches enjoy the tiny seeds produced by water forget-me-nots (see p. 127).

FLAG IRIS
Birds use the long leaves of flag iris as cover (see p. 127).

FLOWERING RUSH
Flowering rush attracts water lily aphids and other insects (see p. 127).

REED
Reed flowers are used by birds as nest material (see p. 119).

BULRUSH
Typha latifolia
These tall plants attract birds with their autumn seedheads. The dead leaves make good nesting material.

WATER LILY
Nymphaea alba
Water lilies grow in sunny sites in deep water. Each spring they produce round leaves and fragrant, white flowers.

SETTING UP A GARDEN POND

POND SIZE AND SHAPE are dictated by the dimensions of the space available, but by using a flexible liner you can tailor both to suit your garden. The best material is butyl rubber, which is expensive but tough and lasts for about 50 years. PVC is cheaper but more likely to tear and may not last more than 10 years.

Your pond needs to receive at least half a day's sunshine daily and, ideally, it should be visible from most points in the garden. The water should be deep enough to protect animals and plants in winter and have a large enough surface area to allow sufficient oxygen exchange. Avoid a site with overhanging trees, especially poisonous laburnum, since the leaves will clutter up the pond. Make sure that your pond has a sloping pebble beach in one corner for birds to bathe and to allow small animals to get in and out of the water. Use the spoil left over from digging out the pond to make a bank or rockery. This will form a sheltering backdrop to the pond and will be ideal for growing plants that prefer dry soil. A small tree or shrub will shelter birds after bathing.

Maintaining a Pond

Like any other part of the garden, ponds need routine care. If the pond is filled with tap water, allow a few days for the chlorine to disperse. Growths of algae can often spoil the appearance of a pond. These can be pulled out with a rake but fish, tadpoles, and other creatures tend to be removed with it. Instead, use a chemical treatment that is harmless to other plants and animals, or stuff old tights with barley (not wheat) straw and sink them in the pond. The rotting straw releases a chemical that inhibits algae. Thick masses of green blanketweed, which develop when a pond is rich in nutrients from soil or rotting leaves, deprives pond animals of valuable oxygen. This can be countered by oxygenating plants such as frogbit, which floats and does not need planting. Duckweed can also clog up ponds and should be removed at regular intervals. Skim the surface with a plank to remove the excess weed, and dispose of it carefully, since it spreads vigorously.

PLANTING BASKETS

Containers make it easy to tend or reposition aquatic plants. Use unfertilized garden soil or aquatic compost, and line wide-mesh baskets with hessian to prevent soil from escaping.

FINE MESH, ROUND

WIDE MESH, CURVED

FINE MESH, SHAPED

FINE MESH, SQUARE

WIDE MESH, LARGE

Preventing Blanketweed
In autumn, lay fine mesh netting across the pond, held in place with pegs or bricks, to catch falling leaves.

MAKING A WATERCOURSE WITH A FLEXIBLE LINER

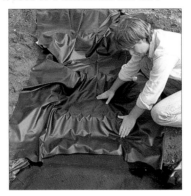

1 *Choose a sloping site or build a soil bank to the required height and mark the shape of the watercourse. Assess the amount of liner needed, based on the route and dimensions.*

2 *Remove any sharp stones and cushion the site with a layer of matting. Position the liner, allowing an overlap on the bottom edge. Cut to fit, leaving 30 cm on each side.*

3 *Smooth the liner into the contours, then set the rocks in place to form steps. Prevent water escaping by tucking the edges of the liner behind the rocks. Backfill firmly with soil.*

4 *Working upwards, form the falls and sides of the watercourse. The sides should be steep enough to prevent water escaping. Bury the pipe alongside to overhang the pool.*

5 *Position plants in the crevices to soften the edges, and hide the end of the pipe with pebbles. A layer of gravel will create a natural finish. Adjust the rocks before cementing them in position. Use a variety of marginals and rock-garden plants, such as ferns, flag irises, and meadow saxifrages, to attract wildlife.*

Chapter Two

CARING FOR YOUR BIRD GARDEN

GARDENING IS AN ONGOING SERIES of tasks, and work in a birdfeeder's garden is no exception. However, it is possible to devise a garden scheme that suits your level of commitment and gardening know-how. This chapter presents basic horticultural advice on what to look for when buying plants and how to grow, maintain, and propagate them successfully.

Once the design and planting scheme for your garden have been planned, the site must be properly prepared. It is easy to lose expensive plants through initial neglect, so after planting, they must be nurtured until they have become well established. Mature gardens need regular maintenance, too. Failed plants need to be replaced or moved to more suitable sites, new varieties might be tried, and special features can be introduced. Whatever the task, it can be carried out in a bird-friendly way to ensure that birds will visit your garden all year round.

Winter Fruits
Fruit-eaters such as waxwings are attracted to gardens that offer berry-laden shrubs and fallen fruits during harsh winter weather.

CHOOSING PLANTS

B EFORE BUYING PLANTS for your garden, make a study of gardening reference books and plant catalogues. This will help you to find species that suit local conditions and that match the requirements of your garden plan.

Mail-order nurseries usually offer a wide range of plants, and some of them specialize in native and wildlife-friendly species. However, good local garden centres are more likely to stock plants that suit the location and soil type of your garden. They also advise on the best varieties to grow and how to cultivate them.

Trees and shrubs can be bought at any size, from seedlings to semi-mature trees. Young plants take longer than more mature specimens to fill out a new garden, but they are often easier to establish. The empty space that surrounds immature plants can be used for interplanting with annuals and biennials, which will bring instant colour and foliage to a site.

Plants are sold in three different conditions: bare-root, root-balled, or container-grown. Plants with no soil around their roots (that is bare-rooted) must be planted when they are dormant in autumn or spring. Large trees and evergreens are often sold as root-balled plants, and have their roots covered in loose soil and enclosed in sacking or netting. These too should be planted between autumn and spring. Container-grown specimens can be planted at any time of the year without disturbing the roots – a great advantage with species that are difficult to establish. To create an "instant" garden, choose from the wide selection of these plants that are available commercially.

Whichever type of plant you choose, check it for good health and vigorous growth. Generally, if a container-grown plant is more than six times taller than the diameter of its pot, it is liable to be pot-bound and weak.

Selecting a Healthy Specimen
When choosing a container-grown shrub, ease the plant out of the pot to check that the roots are not overcrowded.

Vigorous, balanced growth

Soil held firmly around roots

Well-established root system

Choosing a Tree or Shrub
Bare-root plants should be damp, with evenly spread roots around the stem. Look for plenty of small roots, as a sign that the plant has been trimmed regularly to produce good growth.

Fibrous "feeder" roots

Roots spread evenly around stem

Selecting Plant Varieties

Height, spread, soil, and climate are factors that need to be considered when choosing plants. Once you have decided on a species, try to find a variety that best suits the conditions in your garden. Some plants prefer acid soil or tolerate polluted or salty air, while others are particularly good for bird gardens that aim to provide an almost continuous supply of fruits and seedheads. For example, the fruit of the Siberian crab apple (*Malus baccata*) ripens late and remains on the tree during winter, whereas *M.* 'Spring Snow' seldom produces fruit. It is also worth noting that varieties condemned by horticulturists for being susceptible to attack from caterpillars or birds are often the best choices for planting in bird gardens.

Filling out Flowerbeds
Annuals and biennials "fill out" immature beds, but be prepared to lose some of the brightly coloured flowers to house sparrows, who tear the petals to shreds.

Planting in Containers
Add interest to terraces by planting up pots of different shapes and sizes. Birds may use them as perching posts or for nesting. Here, a disused chimney pot is filled with pansies and trailing ivy.

Comparing Varieties
Cultivated varieties of a particular species can differ in size, form, and colour, so it is important to choose plants that best suit your garden. For example, the hill cherry, Prunus jamasakura (left), grows to a height and spread of 12 m, while the fragrant rosebud cherry, Prunus x subhirtella (above), is a weeping variety that grows to only 8 m.

PLANTING AND WATERING

ALL PLANTS BENEFIT from a site that has been well prepared, especially if the plot has been reclaimed from a long-neglected garden. Increase aeration in the soil by digging it over, remove rubble and large stones, and break up any compacted areas. Dig out perennial weeds and completely remove their root systems. Improve the soil structure with well-rotted organic material or, if the soil is very poor, add a slow-release fertilizer.

Watering Correctly

Seedlings, cuttings, and new plantings need regular watering until they have become fully established. It is also best to soak the roots of container-grown plants before planting them out. Whether using a watering can or garden hose, never direct the water at the base of a plant because it may wash away soil, leaving the roots exposed and prone to drying out. Instead, water the soil thoroughly around the plant, pausing to allow "puddles" to soak in.

STORING SEEDS

When clearing an overgrown garden, you can save seeds from plants that have to be removed and store them until you are ready to raise the seedlings.

Collecting Seeds
Shake the dry, ripe seeds from a seedhead and place them in an envelope. Add a label and store the seeds in a cool, dry place.

Extracting Seeds from Berries
Squeeze the berries, then wash the seeds in warm water to remove remaining debris. Tissue-dry the seeds and store them in a plastic bag with a little coarse sand, in a cool place.

PLANTING A PERENNIAL

1 *Dig a hole that is one and a half times wider and deeper than the plant's root-ball. Before planting, soak the pot well for at least 20 minutes.*

2 *Gently slide the plant from its pot, removing the top layer of compost, which may contain weeds. Carefully loosen the ends of the roots.*

3 *Place the plant in the hole, with the crown at ground level. Fill in around the roots, then press the soil firmly. Water the plant in thoroughly.*

PLANTING A TREE OR SHRUB

1 Mark out a hole measuring about three or four times the diameter of the root-ball. Remove any turf or weeds, then dig out the hole to about one and a half times the depth of the root-ball.

2 Loosen the sides and bottom of the hole with a fork. Add well-rotted organic matter and fertilizer to the soil to improve the structure and drainage.

3 If necessary, position a stake off-centre and hammer it into place. Add one-fifth of the soil enriched with organic matter to the hole.

4 Slide the plant from its container and lay it on the ground. Gently tease out the roots and remove any weeds in the soil or damaged roots.

5 Hold the plant next to the stake and spread out the roots. Using a cane, check that the soil mark is level with the surface of the ground.

6 Backfill with soil enriched with organic matter, lifting the plant at intervals so that the soil settles between the roots. Tread firmly around the plant.

7 Fork the soil over lightly, then water the bed well and add a layer of mulch. Cut back any damaged stems or long sideshoots (inset).

STAKING AND PROTECTING

UNTIL THEIR ROOTS become established in the soil, most plants are susceptible to damage by wind, drought, and severe weather. If your garden is on an exposed or coastal site, you will need to support and shelter young plants. Trees and shrubs are particularly vulnerable for the first two or three years after being planted in their new positions.

Supporting Plants

Use canes to support slender or top-heavy plants, such as sunflowers, to ensure that they are not damaged before flowering and seeding. In the vegetable plot, beans, peas, and peppers all need to be trained on upright canes. Make sure that the canes are strong enough to bear the weight of the resultant crops. Climbers are best supported by several canes, one per shoot, until there is sufficient growth to attach and train them up a trellis or pergola.

A young tree or tall shrub should be supported with a stake to anchor the base of the plant. This prevents the root-ball from moving, but still allows the trunk to sway in the wind. Leave the stake in place for two or three years until the tree or shrub is firmly established. To avoid disturbing the roots of a container-grown or root-balled tree, drive in the stake at an angle, facing into the prevailing wind; in very windy sites, place two or three stakes around the tree. Longer stakes that reach up to branch level suit very pliable trees.

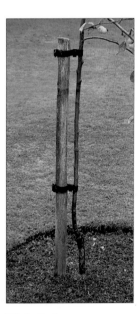

High Stake
Use a high stake on flexible trees in windy sites. Drive the stake into the bottom of a hole before planting. The stake can be removed after two or three years.

Low Stake
For supporting container-grown and root-balled trees, drive in a low stake clear of the root-ball. It will allow the trunk to move freely without the roots working loose.

Single Cane
A weak or fragile, single-stemmed plant may be damaged by the wind. When the plant reaches 20–25 cm, tie it loosely to a single cane.

Ring of Canes
For a clump of weak, multi-stemmed plants, make a circle of several canes and loop twine around the clump to keep the stems from falling.

Fix a tree to the stake with ties that expand, otherwise they will cut into the bark and restrict growth, possibly deforming or killing the tree. Adjust the ties at regular intervals so that pests do not gather underneath.

Providing Protection

The hard work of nurturing a new tree, shrub, or other plant can be lost overnight through the activities of animals. The main culprits are cats, which claw trunks, and rabbits and deer, which chew bark, eat buds and leaves, and graze on low-growing herbaceous plants. This damage distorts a plant's shape and impairs its growth. Protective collars or netting are the best defence for plants that are prone to cat damage. To keep rabbits out of the garden, install 1-m high netting around the boundary, burying it 30 cm in the ground so that they cannot burrow underneath. "Ring-barking", whereby bark is completely stripped from the circumference of a trunk, is often carried out by deer in winter and can kill a tree. Use 2-m fencing to prevent deer from jumping over into your garden. Scatterings of hair clippings or dried blood fertilizer may also deter them.

PROTECTING PLANTS IN WINTER

Delicate or young plants and gardens in exposed sites can be damaged by severe winter weather. Protection against drifting snow, cold winds, and frost reduces the likelihood of plant loss.

Using Hessian and Straw
Working from the bottom up, pack straw around the plant, then loosely wrap in hessian.

Using Windbreaks
Use flexible double netting supported by canes to shelter young plants and fragile stems.

Protecting Stems and Trunks
The simplest protection is provided by tubes of chicken-wire or plastic-coated netting wrapped around the trunk of a shrub or tree. Rigid, degradable plastic guards are available in a range of sizes. A neater solution is provided by plastic spiral collars, which you can purchase from well-stocked garden centres.

WIRE NETTING   RIGID PLASTIC   HEAVY-DUTY RUBBER   SPIRAL COLLAR

TRANSPLANTING AND PROPAGATION

IT IS RARE FOR A GARDEN PLAN to produce perfect results first time around. Often your planting ideas change or the addition of a new feature makes it necessary to alter some areas of the garden. Plants that grow larger than expected need to be transplanted to a new site or divided into smaller plants. Where plants have grown successfully in your garden, you will probably want to increase your stocks.

Moving Plants

Herbaceous perennials lend themselves easily to transplanting and can be kept in dry storage for long periods if packed well. Dig the plants up when dormant in autumn or early spring, making sure that there is plenty of soil around the roots. If a plant has become too large for its site, divide it into smaller clumps and replant them. Moving shrubs or, rarely, trees, is more time consuming. Once moved, larger plants need nurturing, since they can take up to three years to become re-established in a new site.

Increasing Your Stock

An economical and satisfying way of acquiring plants is to propagate them from existing specimens. Perennials need to be lifted and divided every few years. This helps to keep the plants in good shape and prevents them from overcrowding a bed. It also provides an opportunity for clearing a site of obstinate weeds before replanting. To divide a plant, loosen and lever it up with a fork and shake off the soil. Small perennials may simply be pulled apart by hand, keeping the best divisions with shoots and discarding any weaker pieces. Tougher plants with fibrous or woody roots need to be cut with a spade or knife, taking care not to damage the shoots. Replant in an ample hole, with the plant roots fully spread out, then pack soil firmly around the plant.

Shrubs can be propagated from seeds, by division, layering, or grafting, or from cuttings. Although it takes time to produce a plant of flowering size from a fruit or berry, it makes

TRANSPLANTING A SHRUB OR TREE

1 *Tie in any trailing or delicate stems, or wrap the plant in hessian to prevent damage. Using a spade, mark a circle around the width of the plant.*

2 *Dig a trench around the plant, following the marked-out circle. Taking care not to harm the roots, fork soil away from the root-ball.*

a challenging project. Some seeds have a period of dormancy, which ensures that they do not begin to grow in adverse conditions. Germination can be stimulated by soaking the seeds in cold water or by chilling them in a refrigerator. Alternatively, pierce a hole in each seed coat or rub it with glasspaper, to allow air and moisture to penetrate.

Most cuttings are best taken from shrubs in late summer and autumn, or after the leaves have fallen. To produce a healthy, new plant that has a well-developed root system, avoid using a cutting taken from old or weak wood. Instead, look for a fully ripe shoot showing vigorous growth and which is, preferably, on a flowerless stem. Make the cut just below a node or leaf joint, and remove most or all of the leaves from the shoot, as they will demand more water. Some plants, such as willow, can be propagated by simply pushing a cutting into the ground, but most other plants need nurturing. Dip the cutting in hormone rooting powder and plant it in a container of prepared cutting compost. Keep the compost moist until the cutting develops a strong root system.

RAISING FROM SEEDS AND CUTTINGS

Sowing Seeds
Sow seeds thinly in a pot of gritty seed compost that is moist. As the seedlings emerge, thin or "prick" them out into a larger pot or prepared bed.

Taking Cuttings
Remove leaves and trim off any soft wood on the stems. Dip 15-cm lengths into rooting powder and plant in cutting compost.

Layering
Take a section with a root system and new growth, remove the lower leaves, and plant in a pot of cutting compost or in situ.

3 *Undercut the root-ball with a spade to separate the plant from the soil. Place a hessian sheet beneath the plant, tilting the plant from side to side.*

4 *Pull the sheet up around the root-ball and tie it securely around the trunk or stem. Lift the plant carefully out of its hole and move it to the new planting site.*

5 *Remove the sheet and replant the tree or shrub, making sure that soil covers the same parts of the plant as before. Firm the soil, water well, and mulch.*

TRIMMING AND PRUNING

A CAREFUL BALANCE is needed when carrying out maintenance in your bird garden. While plants are best left untended for the benefit of visiting birds, some routine tidying is needed to preserve the appearance of the garden and to promote healthy growth.

Keeping Plants in Shape

Light pruning, or trimming, keeps a plant in shape and encourages healthy growth. One solution for retaining the wildlife value of a shrub or hedge is to cut back part of the growth in alternate years. For example, hedges of privet are usually trimmed two or three times during the growing season. If allowed to grow unchecked through the summer, privet produces tiny flowers, which attract insects, and shiny, black berries that are popular with birds. This makes privet a valuable asset in the birdfeeder's garden but, by autumn, the plant has lost its compactness and looks untidy. More important, the straggly growth makes it a less secure site for nesting. Trimming sections of the hedge in rotation allows the privet to be enjoyed by birds and kept in good shape.

Hedge Trimming
Dense growth can be encouraged by regular trimming, and provides a well-concealed site for nesting and roosting birds. To achieve a smooth outline, keep the blade of the trimmer parallel to the hedge and cut with a wide, sweeping action.

Herbaceous perennials die down after flowering and become very untidy-looking. However, you should try to resist clearing the debris away, because the dead growth bears the seedheads that are needed by birds for autumn and winter food. Remember that dead-heading some plants can promote a second flowering which, in turn, will produce a later crop of seeds. Some shrubby ground cover, including

TRAINING NEW GROWTH

Young trees and hedges need formative pruning in their first and second years of growth. This ensures that they develop balanced branch structures, dense, bushy growth, and good, compact shapes.

Before Pruning
If left unchecked, the new growth of leaders and laterals becomes straggly and the plant loses its compactness and shape.

After Pruning
Bushy growth is ensured by cutting back the laterals by half and by pruning the leaders to the desired height.

heathers, needs to be trimmed occasionally to prevent the stems from falling over and revealing bare, woody centres. Other plants become "leggy" and untidy-looking, when they produce straggling stems and branches. Cut back this unwanted growth regularly to encourage a dense structure of new shoots that gives plants shape and compactness.

Reviving Weak Plants

Hard pruning, where stems are cut short, promotes more vigorous growth than trimming. It is used to revive shrubs that have weak and congested growth and should not be performed on strong, healthy growth. Take care not to kill a plant that has a low tolerance of pruning. The amount of maintenance needed for shrubs depends on whether a species is grown for its flowers, fruits, or foliage. Roses need trimming in autumn to prevent wind damage, followed by hard pruning in spring to stimulate flowering.

PRUNING A DENSE CLIMBER

Before pruning, always check for nesting birds that might be concealed in the foliage and avoid removing any seedheads. The dense mass of thin, twiggy stems produced by climbers needs to be shaped with shears to encourage strong growth in the following year.

PRUNING AN EVERGREEN SHRUB

Spring is the best time for pruning evergreen shrubs, provided that there is no danger of any late, hard frosts. Remove all dead wood where new growth is emerging, and thin out any overcrowded shoots. Do not worry about visible pruning scars since these will be concealed quickly by the season's new foliage. Once the flowering is over, any flowered stems, damaged wood, or straggly growth can be cut back to retain the plant's shape.

Removing Dead Wood
For a sound framework of branches and healthy growth, remove all diseased, dead, or damaged wood as it appears. Cut back to the plant base, if necessary.

Cutting Back Awkward Stems
Stems that emerge at awkward angles hinder a balanced structure. Cut them back to well-positioned, healthy shoots that are facing outwards from the plant.

Dead-heading Flowered Stems
After flowering, dead-head all flowering stems, then cut them back to a main stem or outwards-facing bud. Remove any thickly congested or crossing stems.

CONTROLLING WEEDS AND PESTS

MANY GARDEN WEEDS, such as thistles and dandelions, produce seedheads that are attractive to birds but they can present a serious problem for bird gardeners. While you may want to let some weeds flourish to attract goldfinches and greenfinches, it is important to know how to contain the resulting colony.

Keeping Weeds at Bay

Weeds are vigorous growers and spread rapidly, often smothering cultivated plants and sending down deep roots that make them difficult to eliminate. Annual weeds such as clover and groundsel are easy to clear by hoeing the seedlings or hand–pulling fully grown plants. Perennial weeds such as ground elder, bindweed, stinging nettle, thistle, and bramble are more difficult to eradicate because of their

Timber frame

Alternating layers of manure and waste material

Making Good Use of Waste
Grass clippings, kitchen waste, and weeds can all be added to garden compost. Mixed with a proprietary compost activator and turned regularly to circulate air, the materials decompose and can be used within three to four months.

USING MULCHES AND SOIL ADDITIVES

When preparing a new site or restoring one that has become overgrown, ensure that the soil contains enough nutrients to support strong plant growth. Dig in organic material and soil additives, which help to improve the soil structure and ensure good water retention.

Mushroom Compost
A valuable fertilizer and soil improver, mushroom compost is alkaline and therefore not suitable for acid-loving plants.

Mulching
Using compost, bark chippings, or other organic materials, apply a 5-cm layer of mulch around plants to retain moisture in the soil and deter weeds. Avoid mulching in winter when the soil is still cold or frozen.

Manure
Well-rotted animal manure encourages earthworms, which improve aeration and drainage in the soil.

Coconut Fibre
This soil improver can be used as a substitute for peat. It is particularly effective for increasing water retention in soil.

deep roots. These often form an underground system of well-established weeds, since each small piece of storage organ left in the soil sprouts into a new plant. The best solution is repeated forking, which weakens and eventually eliminates the most persistent weeds.

When planting a new bed, dig the site over thoroughly to aerate the soil and ensure a weed-free start. Any reinvasion of weeds can then be checked by regular hoeing, mulching, and planting ground cover. Organic mulches are an attractive solution for the bird garden, because they support a rich fauna of small animals. This, in turn, attracts ground-feeding birds, especially blackbirds, which enjoy foraging through the organic material. Use the fallen leaves collected in the autumn clear-up of the garden as a natural mulch on flowerbeds to enrich the soil and protect plants during winter. Inorganic mulches are useful for large, fallow beds and vegetable plots. Cover the

Earwigs shelter in pots during daytime

Trapping Earwigs
Earwigs destroy the young leaves of many garden plants. To lure and trap these pests, fill a pot with dried grass and invert it on a cane. Destroy all contents of the pot every two days.

surface of the soil with pieces of old carpet, polythene or plastic sheets, foil, or gravel, and conceal with a thin layer of decorative mulch or leaf litter to achieve a natural-looking finish.

Dealing with Pests

Healthy populations of caterpillars, aphids, and other larvae are appreciated by birds with families to feed, but can devastate a garden. Nevertheless, it is possible to combat pests without resorting to chemical sprays. Caterpillars can simply be removed by hand, and natural insecticides, such as pyrethrum or soap-based sprays, offer efficient pest control. To evict leatherjackets from your lawn, water the area well and cover it with a black plastic sheet. Remove the leatherjackets from under the sheet as they are forced to the surface or leave them as a feast for the birds. Slugs are among the most persistent pests in the garden. Thrushes and hedgehogs both feed on them but their efforts are unlikely to have a serious effect on slug populations. If your garden is being overrun by these pests, use commercial slug pellets that are harmless to predators.

Defending Neighbouring Plants
*Plants that are attractive to predatory insects can be used to encourage natural pest control in a flowerbed. For example, French marigolds (*Tagetes patula*) attract hoverflies, which will feed on any aphids that may be attacking nearby plants.*

Chapter Three

MAKING A HOME
FOR BIRDS

T HE BIRDFEEDER'S GARDEN becomes an exciting place for watching birds if they can be invited to nest. Many of the birds that feed in urban areas in winter return to the countryside to breed because nesting sites are more plentiful there than in gardens. However, this lack of nesting places can be remedied.

Nestboxes will attract a variety of cavity-nesting birds, especially tits, to a garden, while careful pruning of trees and shrubs will provide sites to attract birds that build nests in the open. One important advantage of artificial nesting sites is that they offer better protection to birds than many of the nests in natural sites, which are often damaged or completely destroyed by bad weather or predators.

This chapter outlines what birds need in the nesting season, and gives practical advice on how you can build your own nestboxes, provide artificial nesting sites, and protect nesting birds.

Garden Nestbox
Great tits and other members of the tit family are cavity-nesting birds, and will readily take up residence in enclosed nestboxes.

USING NESTBOXES

Tits, starlings, nuthatches, and redstarts all use natural cavities for nesting, but these are often in short supply in gardens. Nestboxes are eagerly accepted by birds as substitute nesting sites and encourage them to become garden residents. Ready-made boxes are available from specialist suppliers, pet shops, and garden centres, but home-made versions can be built easily from timber scraps. If well constructed, nestboxes last longer and offer better protection against rain than nests which, when sodden, can kill nestlings.

Securing Nestboxes

Nestboxes can be attached directly to tree trunks or suspended from branches or brackets. Remember to check fixings annually for deterioration and replace any worn or damaged parts. Ties should be slackened regularly, otherwise they may inhibit a tree's growth.

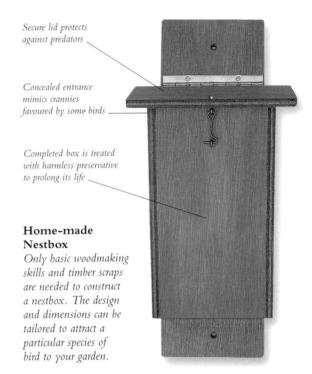

Secure lid protects against predators

Concealed entrance mimics crannies favoured by some birds

Completed box is treated with harmless preservative to prolong its life

Home-made Nestbox
Only basic woodmaking skills and timber scraps are needed to construct a nestbox. The design and dimensions can be tailored to attract a particular species of bird to your garden.

CHOOSING READY-MADE NESTBOXES

A wide range of ready-made nestboxes is available, from mock manor houses to simple log boxes. Although ornamental boxes may look attractive, they are often poorly constructed and do not cater fully for the needs of nesting birds. Equally, unnecessary decoration on the outside of the box may deter birds from using it for nesting. A feeding tray is not desirable on a nestbox, because its contents may attract unwanted visitors to the nest. When choosing a nestbox, make sure that it is made from weatherproof material, such as durable plastic, or wood that has been treated with a non-toxic preservative. Check also that the nestbox does not have any ill-fitting panels that can let water into the nest.

Sturdy fixing bar

Removable lid allows nestbox to be cleaned

Small entrance hole keeps out large birds

Rough bark gives good toe-hold for birds using nestbox

Gabled Box
Although a sloping roof tends to restrict air circulation inside a nestbox, it offers effective protection against rain.

Log Box
A hollowed-out log makes a useful nestbox for woodland birds and blends in well in a garden setting.

Working Safely

Take care when putting up nestboxes. Make sure that ladders are securely placed before mounting them. Look out for power cables, either overhead or concealed within a structure in which you are inserting nails or screws.

Once a nestbox has been adopted by a family of birds as their home, try not to disrupt them. If you need to approach a nesting site, do so with care, since birds often desert their nests before completion if they are disturbed. Owls, in particular, can be aggressive at their nests and may attack with their talons. Wear goggles, a hat, and thick clothing as protection.

Removing Disused Nests

Disused nests must be removed after the nesting season, because they can host parasites and disease that will infect the next generation of birds. Make sure that a nest is no longer being used by birds before clearing it away, and be prepared to find addled eggs and dead nestlings, even in nests that were successful.

FEATHERS

MOSS

CATTLE HAIR

GRASS

LICHEN

Nest Material
Some birds do not make nests inside nestboxes. Others gather material such as grass, feathers, lichen, moss, and hair to insulate the nestbox.

SITING NESTBOXES

There is no guarantee that a nestbox will attract birds, but careful siting increases the likelihood of it being used for nesting. Birdsong heard nearby is a good indication that a bird is looking for a place to nest. Some nestboxes are occupied almost immediately, while others may not be adopted until several years after they have been installed. If a nestbox remains ignored after three or four years, try moving it to a different location. You could also try using a different type of nestbox that has been designed to appeal to a particular species. Occasionally, bumblebees or wasps occupy nestboxes, but this lasts only until the end of summer, when the colonies become extinct.

Although the fixing height of a box is generally not important, some birds prefer to nest high away from any disturbance. It is best to site nestboxes just before nesting starts in spring. However, a nestbox installed in autumn may attract birds such as tits, which roost during winter. Look for a pile of droppings below the nestbox as a sign of roosting birds. You can reserve nestboxes for migrant birds returning in spring by plugging the entrances, so that other birds cannot move in.

Sheltered Site
A nestbox should be positioned in a site that is safe from predators, especially cats, and not too exposed. There should also be a clear flight path to the entrance.

MAKING NESTBOXES

ONE OF THE BENEFITS of making your own nestbox is that you can tailor it to suit a particular species of garden bird. Listed below are the recommended dimensions for the two types of standard nestbox – open and enclosed. While the size of a nestbox is not critical, it must not be too small or the nestlings will become cramped. Make sure that the floor measures at least 100 sq cm and check that enclosed nestboxes are deep enough to keep out predators. Do not worry that nestlings will be trapped inside; they will have no difficulty in scrambling up the steep sides when it is time for them to leave the nestbox.

Useful Tips

For adequate insulation in a nestbox, use wood that is at least 15 mm thick. Treat the exterior with a non-toxic preservative to extend the life of the box. A hinged lid is useful to allow the nestbox to be cleaned out.

A sloping roof is not necessary, especially if the box is tilted forwards at an angle so that rain does not fall in the entrance. Waterproof the box by sealing the joints with glue or mastic. Drill small drainage holes in the bottom of the box to prevent waterlogging and add a second set of holes near the top to improve ventilation during hot weather.

RECOMMENDED NESTBOX DIMENSIONS

	Bird Species	Floor Size	Box Depth	Hole/Entrance	Comments
ENCLOSED	Great tit	15 × 12 cm	12 cm to hole	3-cm diameter	Place in a sheltered site.
	House sparrow	15 × 15 cm	15 cm to hole	3.5-cm diameter	Place in a sheltered site.
	Jackdaw	20 × 20 cm	40 cm to hole	15-cm diameter	Place in a high, secluded position.
	Little owl	30 × 30 cm	30 cm to hole	7-cm diameter	Partition the box to darken the hole.
	Mallard	30 × 30 cm	20 cm to hole	15-cm diameter	Position on a raft or island.
	Nuthatch	15 × 15 cm	12 cm to hole	3.5-cm diameter	Place in a sheltered site.
	Pied flycatcher	13 × 13 cm	20 cm to hole	3-cm diameter	Block entrance until birds arrive.
	Redstart	13 × 13 cm	20 cm to hole	3.5-cm diameter	Place in a sheltered site.
	Ring-necked parakeet	25 × 25 cm	80 cm to hole	8 cm–diameter	Place high on a tree or building.
	Starling	15 × 15 cm	30 cm to hole	5.5-cm diameter	Place in a sheltered site.
	Street pigeon	20 × 20 cm	10 cm to hole	10-cm diameter	Add an outside perch.
	Tits (excl. Great tit)	15 × 12 cm	12 cm to hole	2.5-cm diameter	Place in a sheltered site.
	Woodpeckers	15 × 15 cm	40 cm to hole	6-cm diameter	Fill to entrance with polystyrene.
OPEN-FRONTED	Black redstart	10 × 10 cm	15 cm	5 cm	Place in a sheltered site.
	Kestrel	30 × 50 cm	30 cm	10 cm	Fix on 5-m pole. Add outside perch.
	Redstart	13 × 13 cm	15 cm	11 cm	Place in a sheltered site.
	Robin	10 × 10 cm	15 cm	5 cm	Place in a sheltered site.
	Tawny owl	25 × 25 cm	80 cm	60 cm	Add an outside perch.
	Wren	10 × 10 cm	15 cm	10 cm	Place in a sheltered site.

STANDARD NESTBOX

Both the open-fronted and enclosed versions of the standard nestbox are used by a variety of garden birds. These boxes serve as substitutes for small tree holes, which are often in short supply. An enclosed nestbox has a central entrance hole in a full-length panel and appeals to most small garden birds, while an open-fronted nestbox has a half-length front panel and is commonly used by robins and flycatchers.

Constructing the nestbox

Draw the outline of each panel on the wood, measuring carefully with a ruler, then saw out the panels. To make the entrance hole for an enclosed nestbox, use an adjustable bit or mark out and drill a circle of holes on the front panel, and join them up with a fretsaw. Use the metal plate or tin lid to

reinforce the hole against squirrels and woodpeckers, filing down any rough edges. Saw one of the short sides of the lid at an angle, so that it fits tightly to the back of the box. Before assembling the box, drill small attachment holes at the top and bottom of the back panel. Nail the side panels to the 150-mm sides of the base, then add the front and back panels. For the open-fronted box, nail the lid to the top of the side panels. For the enclosed box, use a strip of waterproof material and tacks or a metal hinge to attach the lid to the back panel, and secure it with a hook and eye on each side panel.

Completed Standard Nestboxes
These types of nestbox provide secure nesting sites for a range of garden birds, from treecreepers and redstarts to woodpeckers and tits.

ENCLOSED NESTBOX

OPEN-FRONTED NESTBOX

MATERIALS

- 15-mm thick floorboard or plywood
- Metal plate or tin lid to reinforce hole on enclosed nestbox
- Metal hinge or strip of waterproof material for nestbox lid
- Rustproof tacks, 38-mm nails, hooks, and eyes

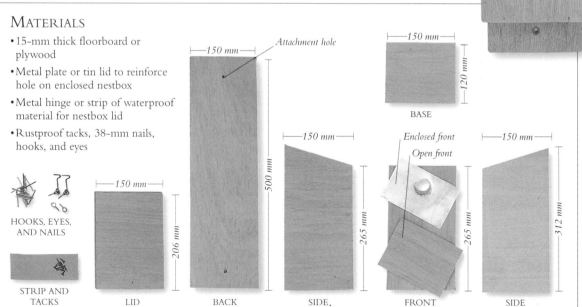

HOOKS, EYES, AND NAILS

STRIP AND TACKS

LID — 150 mm — 206 mm

BACK — 150 mm — 500 mm — Attachment hole

SIDE — 150 mm — 265 mm

FRONT — Enclosed front / Open front — 265 mm

SIDE — 150 mm — 312 mm

BASE — 150 mm — 120 mm

CHIMNEY BOX

Several designs of nestbox have proved successful in imitating natural tree cavities. These types of box attract birds such as tawny owls, which do not build their own nests but lay their eggs in tree holes or in nests abandoned by crows or squirrels. The chimney box is designed to imitate the hollow stump of a tree branch, a popular nesting site for owls. Jackdaws, tawny owls, and kestrels may use chimney boxes in gardens with plenty of mature trees, or open-fronted standard nestboxes (*see p. 67*) where trees have yet to develop hollows or large branches. Owls may also use chimney boxes for sleeping in the daytime.

Before putting up the nestbox, spread a thick layer of sawdust over the box floor. This will absorb any fouling by nestlings, which may otherwise cause the nestbox to rot.

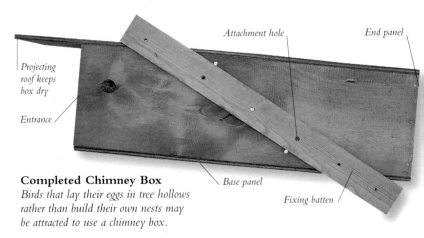

Projecting roof keeps box dry

Entrance

Attachment hole

End panel

Base panel

Fixing batten

Completed Chimney Box
Birds that lay their eggs in tree hollows rather than build their own nests may be attracted to use a chimney box.

Constructing the Nestbox

Draw a pencil outline of the side and end panels on timber, and the roof and base panels on ply, then cut out the panels. Drill a series of small holes in the end panel for drainage. Nail the two sides to the edges of the end panel, then add the base and the roof, making sure that the roof overhangs the entrance so as to keep the box dry. Drill attachment holes in the batten so that it can be screwed to the box. Site the nestbox as high as possible in a tree, and use straps or coated wire, not nails, to fix the batten to the side or underside of a main branch. The box needs to be held securely at an angle of at least 45 degrees to the horizontal.

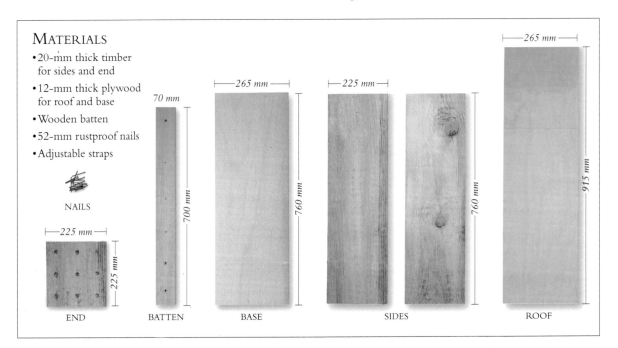

MATERIALS

- 20-mm thick timber for sides and end
- 12-mm thick plywood for roof and base
- Wooden batten
- 52-mm rustproof nails
- Adjustable straps

NAILS

225 mm

225 mm

END

70 mm

700 mm

BATTEN

265 mm

760 mm

BASE

225 mm

760 mm

SIDES

265 mm

915 mm

ROOF

SWIFT BOX

Almost all swifts site their nests in buildings. They prefer to use older properties, since modern houses often lack entrances to the roof space. This presents a problem for swifts in areas where old buildings are being replaced and urban redevelopment is under way, although property developers can sometimes be persuaded to incorporate nesting holes for swifts in new buildings.

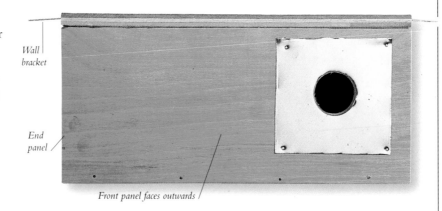

Wall bracket

End panel

Front panel faces outwards

Constructing the Nestbox

Draw pencil outlines of the panels on the wood before cutting them out with a saw. Make the entrance by drilling a circle of holes in the front panel and joining them up with a fretsaw. Reinforce the entrance with the metal plate, filing down any rough metal edges. Using nails, join all of the panels to form a rectangular box.

Screw a wall bracket to each end of the box, making sure that the front panel is facing outwards.

The best site for swift boxes is under the roof eaves, but you must be prepared to wait several years for swifts to find the box. When the swifts have left the nestbox, remove the abandoned nest since it is likely to contain

Completed Swift Box

Swift boxes should be placed as high as possible, under eaves or on gable ends. This allows swifts to launch themselves and gather speed when leaving the nest.

large numbers of insects. Conceal or plug the entrance hole until the spring to prevent house sparrows from occupying the vacant box.

MATERIALS

- 20-mm thick plywood or floorboard
- 52-mm rustproof nails
- 2 L-shaped wall brackets to hold the nestbox in position
- Metal plate to reinforce entrance hole

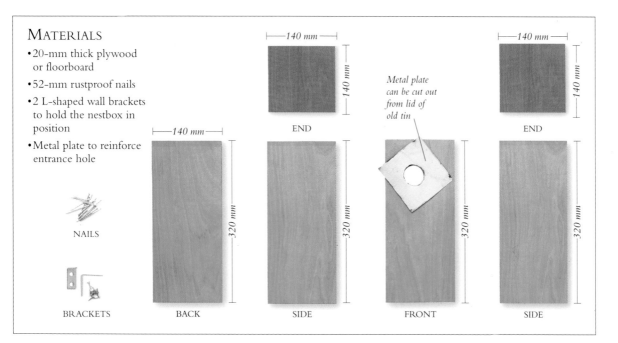

NAILS

BRACKETS

BACK

├─ 140 mm ─┤
END
140 mm

SIDE
320 mm

Metal plate can be cut out from lid of old tin

FRONT
320 mm

├─ 140 mm ─┤
END
140 mm

SIDE
320 mm

├─ 140 mm ─┤
320 mm

TREECREEPER BOX

The treecreeper box is designed to imitate the natural nesting places of treecreepers. These birds prefer well-wooded gardens, where they can nest in tree crevices, under loose pieces of bark or, sometimes, in dense vegetation. To provide a simple nesting hole in your garden that may attract treecreepers, look for a tree with a deep hollow in its trunk. With the bark facing outwards, place a strip of curved bark over the recess and wire it to the trunk. While these artificial sites may be used by treecreepers when natural nesting sites are scarce, they are often subject to attack by predators. A treecreeper nestbox is a more elaborate and stronger alternative. To increase the likelihood of your success in attracting treecreepers, set out several nestboxes in different sites around your garden.

Constructing the Nestbox

Measure and draw the outline of each panel on the wood before cutting out the pieces. Saw one of the long sides of each side panel at an angle for a neat fit. Cut a 2.5-cm diameter semicircle about one-third along the other long edge of each side panel. Use a rasp to curve the long side of each end panel to ensure that the nestbox is a snug fit when fixed against a tree trunk. Assemble the box by nailing the two side panels to the end panel, making sure that the angled sides meet to form a ridge, then add the second end panel. Screw mirror plates to both end panels. Imitate the surface of a tree trunk by gluing strips of bark to the sides of the nestbox. Use wire to strap the box to the trunk of a large, rough-barked tree, at between 1 m and 3 m from the ground.

— Mirror plate

Completed Treecreeper Box

This two-sided nestbox mimics the natural nesting sites of treecreepers by using a tree trunk or branch to provide the rear panel of the box.

MATERIALS

- 20-mm thick plywood or floorboard
- 52-mm rustproof nails
- 2 rustproof mirror plates
- Strips of bark
- Plastic-coated wire

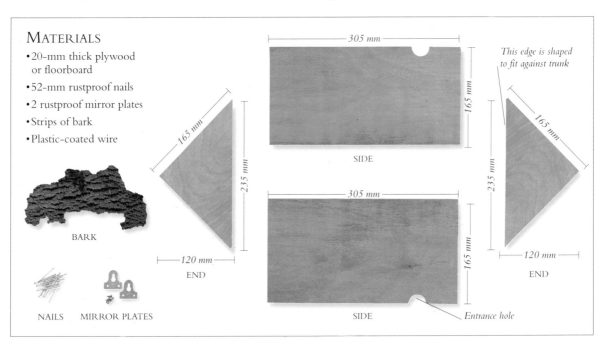

BARK

NAILS   MIRROR PLATES

165 mm

235 mm

120 mm

END

305 mm

165 mm

SIDE

305 mm

165 mm

SIDE

This edge is shaped to fit against trunk

165 mm

235 mm

120 mm

END

— Entrance hole

BOWL NEST

House martins usually nest in traditional colonies, but they can be attracted to new sites where artificial nests, such as bowl nests, are provided. It is best to put up several bowls together, although the birds may build their own mud bowls alongside. Protect nearby windows and paths from droppings by fixing a board underneath the nests. Once the house martins have left, plug the holes to keep out house sparrows.

Constructing the Bowl Nest

Draw the bowl outline, that is, one-quarter of a sphere, on to the ball, and mark an entrance, 6 cm across and 2.5 cm deep, at the top. Mould the papier maché, plaster, or cement, over the section drawn on the ball to a depth of 1 cm and embed a mirror plate on either side of the bowl. Smooth the wet

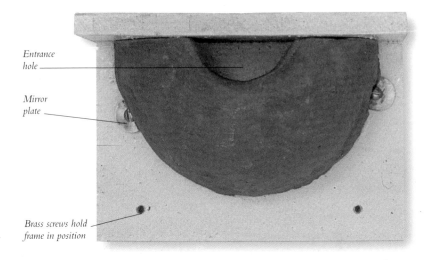

Entrance hole

Mirror plate

Brass screws hold frame in position

material with an old knife as it dries. Nail the two wooden panels to make an L-shaped frame. When the bowl is fully dry, file or trim both edges to fit the frame, and screw it in place. Use brass screws to fix the frame at the nesting site.

Completed Bowl Nest

This type of nest is likely to be successful in attracting house martins if it is placed in a site previously used by the birds for nesting. Swallows may use bowl nests sited in sheds or frameless bowls placed below roof eaves to form open nests.

MATERIALS

- 20-mm thick plywood or hardboard
- Papier maché, made with strips of newspaper and paste; or plaster of Paris or quick-drying cement
- 2 rustproof mirror plates and nails
- Beach ball or similar, with 125-mm diameter or more, to be used as mould

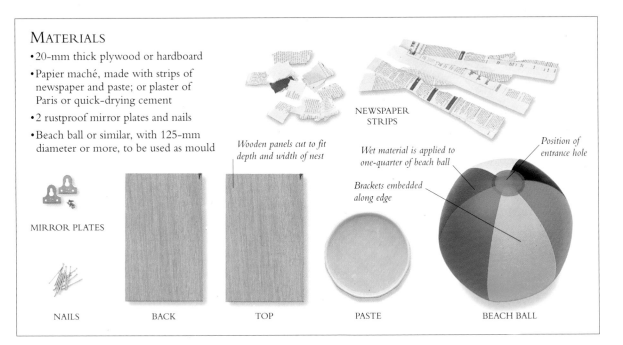

NEWSPAPER STRIPS

MIRROR PLATES

NAILS

BACK

TOP

Wooden panels cut to fit depth and width of nest

Wet material is applied to one-quarter of beach ball

Brackets embedded along edge

Position of entrance hole

PASTE

BEACH BALL

DUCK ISLAND AND BOX

If your garden pond is large enough, an island or raft can be installed to provide cover for nesting ducks and moorhens. Small islands can be made by ballasting large flowerpots, concrete sewer pipes, or old car tyres with rubble, topped with gravel and soil. Provide sloping access to the island, especially if the water is deep at one end, and add marginal plants as cover, and small trees if space allows, to make a natural setting for the island.

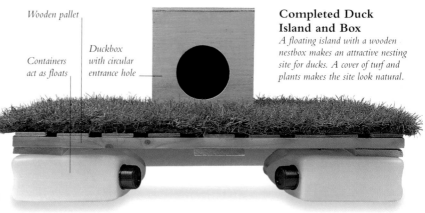

Wooden pallet

Containers act as floats

Duckbox with circular entrance hole

Completed Duck Island and Box
A floating island with a wooden nestbox makes an attractive nesting site for ducks. A cover of turf and plants makes the site look natural.

Constructing the Island

Evenly space the slim timbers across the width of the wooden pallet, and nail them in position to form a secure base for the island. Nail the wire netting to this base, then add the layer of turf and press it into the netting to hold it in place. Using rotproof straps, attach the plastic containers or bags of expanded polystyrene to the underside of the island. Adjust their depth in the water by filling them with ballast such as soil or gravel. Float the island on the water and tether it to a fixed point on land with a rope or chain attached to each side of the base.

Constructing the Box

Measure and draw the outlines of six 30- x 30-cm panels on 20-mm timber. Cut out the pieces and make a 15-cm diameter circle in one panel for an entrance. Nail the sides together to form a cube. Secure the duckbox on the island with two nails through the base.

MATERIALS

- Wooden pallet, approximately 1 m²
- 10 slim timbers to fit pallet
- Wire netting to fit pallet
- Turf to fit pallet
- 4 plastic containers; or bags of expanded polystyrene
- Length of rope or chain
- Rustproof nails
- 20-mm thick timber for box

TURF

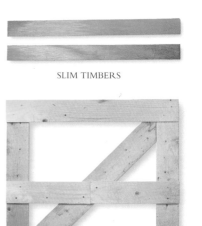

SLIM TIMBERS

Artificial, rot-proof fibre

NAILS

PLASTIC CONTAINER

WIRE NETTING

ROPE

PALLET

BIRD SHELF

Some birds need little more than a firm base on which to build their nests. For example, swallows have been known to support their nests on single projecting nails. A bird shelf provides a more reliable nest base and reduces the likelihood of a nest collapsing and spilling its contents. Spotted flycatchers and pied wagtails will use a bird shelf in an open site from which they have a clear view from the nest. Blackbirds sometimes use an open bird shelf (that is, a box without a lid or front panel), in the same way as they nest on sills.

Constructing the Bird Shelf

Using dimensions from the chart below, draw pencil outlines of each panel on the wood and cut out the pieces. Nail the back and front panels to the base, then add the side panels. Position and nail the roof so that it overhangs to keep out rain. Screw a mirror plate to the back of the shelf.

Completed Bird Shelf

The exposed fronts of bird shelves attract birds that like to have a clear view of their surroundings so that they can keep a look out for danger and escape quickly.

Mirror plate

BIRD SHELF DIMENSIONS

Bird Species	Floor Size	Box Depth	Front Panel	Comments
Blackbird	20 x 20 cm	20 cm	2.5 cm	Place in thick cover.
Pied wagtail	10 x 10 cm	10 cm	3 cm	Place low, on a wall.
Spotted flycatcher	15 x 15 cm	10 cm	3 cm	Position with an open view.

MATERIALS

Bird shelf measurements used are for a pied wagtail

• 15-mm thick plywood
• Rustproof screws and long nails to fix wooden panels
• Mirror plate

Sloping edges should be kept at top end of side panels when assembling nestbox

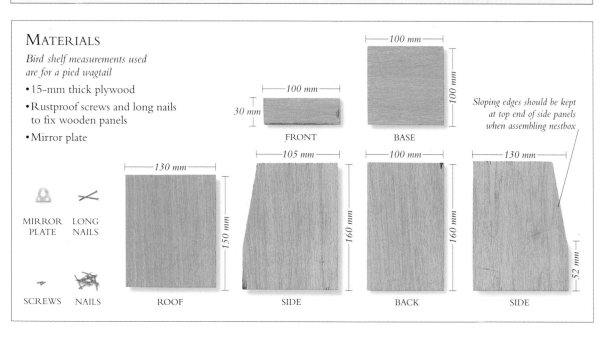

MIRROR PLATE   LONG NAILS

SCREWS   NAILS

FRONT — 100 mm, 30 mm

BASE — 100 mm, 100 mm

ROOF — 130 mm, 150 mm

SIDE — 105 mm, 160 mm

BACK — 100 mm, 160 mm

SIDE — 130 mm, 52 mm

PROVIDING NESTING HABITATS

PUTTING UP NESTBOXES is just one way of making your garden attractive to nesting birds. In fact, only a few bird species can be persuaded to use nestboxes and, of these few, most pairs are more likely to nest in natural surroundings. When you see birds making an intense examination of the trees and hedges in your garden, they are probably searching for a well-concealed site with a good foundation on which to build their nest. To help birds to find the best nest site, you can encourage dense thickets of twigs and a strong branch structure by trimming hedges and trees (*see p. 58*). When training and shaping a shrub or hedge, cut off some of the main stems to force the growth of a solid base. Prune the ring of new stems that sprouts in the following year to produce a cradle. Evergreen trees and hedges are the

MIXED LEAF LITTER

Recycled Litter
Garden litter, such as fallen leaves, seedheads, discarded nut shells, and broken twigs, makes valuable nesting material for birds.

BEECH LITTER

wisest choice for nests that are built early in the season before other trees are in leaf, since nests that are made among bare twigs are more likely to be found by predators.

Coppiced Stool
A low nesting site can be made by coppicing a young tree. To produce a dense cluster of shoots, cut all of the growth back to about 6–8 cm above ground, without damaging the base of the tree.

CREATING AN ARTIFICIAL THICKET

If your garden lacks suitable nesting sites for birds or has yet to mature, artificial thickets are a simple way of providing cover.

1 *Gather sticks or lopped branches of conifers and tie them together tightly in a bundle. Gently tease them out to form a cavity suitable for a nest.*

2 *Fix the bundle to a tree trunk or post in a sheltered site. Train ivy or another climber over it to improve its camouflage and appearance.*

DEFENDING AGAINST PREDATORS

SADLY, MANY CLUTCHES of eggs do not result in families of fledglings. It is estimated that about 90 per cent of nesting attempts by blackbirds and other open-nesters end in failure. Hole-nesting birds, such as great tits, are more successful, with a loss rate of just 30 per cent. Inexperienced parents sometimes simply desert the nest, or cold weather and a shortage of food may force adult birds to abandon the nest. Predators are an ever-present problem during the nesting season.

Little can be done to protect open nests from predatory birds except to encourage thick foliage. Occasionally, it is possible to arrange netting over a bush to shelter a nest from magpies. Hole-nests, including nestboxes, are safe from egg robbers, but woodpeckers, crows, and even owls may take nestlings that climb up to the nest entrance to wait for food. Cats are a particular nuisance in gardens because they are quick and agile enough to catch birds as they enter or leave nestboxes. Grey squirrels often enlarge the holes of nestboxes and pull

Woodcrete Box
A ready-made product, this durable nestbox is made from a mixture of sawdust and concrete. The box keeps out woodpeckers and squirrels, which can bore or enlarge holes in wooden nestboxes to reach nestlings.

Removable door allows old nests to be cleared away

out the nestlings. Remember, too, that humans can, unintentionally, cause birds to abandon their nests. Sparrows, redstarts, treecreepers, and swifts are all easily disturbed and it is best to keep away from their nests when occupied.

PROVIDING NESTBOX DEFENCES

A collar of wire netting or gorse around a tree trunk will often deter predators from raiding a nestbox. Alternatively, several commercial deterrents are available and have proved to be effective in protecting nests.

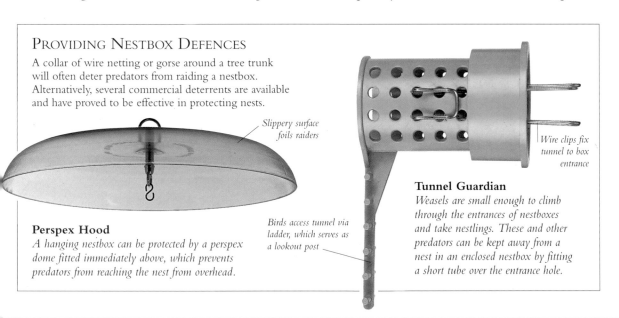

Slippery surface foils raiders

Wire clips fix tunnel to box entrance

Perspex Hood
A hanging nestbox can be protected by a perspex dome fitted immediately above, which prevents predators from reaching the nest from overhead.

Birds access tunnel via ladder, which serves as a lookout post

Tunnel Guardian
Weasels are small enough to climb through the entrances of nestboxes and take nestlings. These and other predators can be kept away from a nest in an enclosed nestbox by fitting a short tube over the entrance hole.

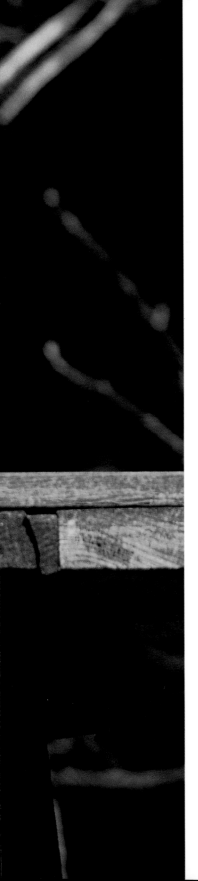

Chapter Four

FEEDING BIRDS

Putting out food is the easiest and quickest way of attracting birds into your garden. When a new garden is started, a tubular feeder, birdtable, or ground-scattered food will tempt bird visitors. Later, when the garden is established with seed- and fruit-bearing plants, this kind of food is still needed to supplement natural foods. This chapter examines the range of feeders and foods that are attractive to birds. It also shows you how to make a birdtable and seed hopper, gives advice on maintaining feeding sites, and suggests how to protect them from unwelcome visitors.

Some birds use birdtables but not feeders, or vice versa, while certain species, such as goldcrests, bullfinches, and treecreepers, which once shunned all artificial feeding sites, are now learning to use them. A birdfeeder has the added advantage of bringing birds to a position where they can be observed easily. When placed outside your window, it will provide a steady source of interest, especially if you have to spend long periods of time indoors.

Nut Feast

Jays will occasionally visit garden birdtables, taking peanuts and kitchen scraps. They are well known for hoarding surplus food.

Feeding Through the Seasons

ORNITHOLOGICAL STUDIES show that birds need to be helped all through the year. Although they are able to survive long periods of freezing weather, garden birds must have access to plenty of food. If a shortage occurs, caused by snow cover, drought, or a late spring, then small birds especially are likely to perish.

Autumn
Bird populations are at their highest in autumn, boosted by the new generation of young birds produced during the summer. Plenty of food is available for birds at this time, since most crops of fruits have ripened. Insects may still be found if the weather remains good, although some insect-eaters transfer to eating fruits in autumn. Migrants need a good supply of food to help them build up reserves for the long journey ahead; sometimes, they may delay their departure for southern climates if supplementary food is provided. In spring, birds that have migrated are keen to return home and nest, but the autumn migration of birds usually adopts a more leisurely pace.

Winter
Traditionally, winter is the time for birdfeeding, because this is when natural supplies start to run low. Insects either die or hibernate when the weather turns cold, and the recent crops of seeds and fruits are gradually used up. Birds are adept at finding new sources of food, and a hopper, peanut feeder, or birdtable soon draws regular visitors. When birds are absent from a garden, it usually means that they are living comfortably elsewhere. Coal tits remain in woodland until food sources are exhausted, and they are unlikely to visit gardens at all in mild

Autumn Harvest
Newly harvested fields provide an abundant supply of fresh seeds for birds, such as this pheasant, to enjoy.

Winter Bounty
Scattered food in the garden draws visitors such as blackbirds in winter, when heavy snow covers the ground.

Nesting Time
Spring marks the start of the nesting season. These blackcaps have returned from their winter home to nest.

Summer Pickings
The abundant supply of fruits and insects in summer helps song thrushes to meet the demands of their hungry nestlings.

winters. In contrast, it is common for siskins and greenfinches to take peanuts and sunflower seeds from feeders even when crops of seeds are still plentiful. Winters can be spectacular for birdwatchers in years when severe food shortages prompt flocks of unusual visitors, such as waxwings and crossbills, to invade gardens. Cold weather may also draw rare visitors such as bramblings and reed buntings.

Spring

Fine weather in spring is important for resident birds that have survived the winter, as well as for migrants arriving from warmer countries. Prolonged spells of cold or wet weather, or the late arrival of spring, can seriously delay the much-needed supply of fresh food. Many of the birds that ate seeds and fruits during winter transfer to eating insects and other small animals in spring and summer.

Summer

Supplementary feeding of birds in summer is now recommended by bird conservation and welfare groups. Together with the abundant supply of naturally occurring foods, such as insects and summer fruits, it helps adult birds to meet the demands of their hungry nestlings. Juicy fruits are especially valuable during periods of hot weather. Avoid putting out very dry foods, such as coconut or stale bread, and always grate whole nuts, because all of these foods may choke nestlings. Most garden birds, including seed-eating finches, also feed their young on insects. Blue tits can often be seen taking caterpillars for their nestlings and, shortly afterwards, returning to the garden to feed on peanuts to boost their own energy levels. An easily found feeding site is a great help to young birds when they have left their nests and are learning to fend for themselves.

CHOOSING FEEDERS

A WIDE CHOICE OF READY-MADE feeders is available, ranging from the simple to the very sophisticated. They can be attached to birdtables or hung from posts or walls in your garden. Other models can be attached to windows, allowing closer observation of birds visiting your garden. Home-made versions of birdtables and seed hoppers can be constructed from leftover pieces of timber and adapted for a particular feeding site in your garden.

Using Window and Hanging Feeders

The introduction of tubular feeders has revolutionized birdfeeding in the garden. They are simple to maintain and keep stocked and draw many more birds into the garden than would be attracted to a birdtable. To observe birds at very close quarters, or if you do not have access to a garden or terrace,

choose a model that can be attached to a window. These types of feeder are fitted either with suction pads that adhere to window panes, or with brackets that enable the feeder to be fitted to a windowsill or frame. Peanut feeders have a metal mesh that is designed to restrict birds to peck small pieces of nuts rather than take whole ones, which may choke young birds. Seed feeders are made from transparent plastic and evenly dispense sunflower seeds and ready-prepared birdfeeder mixes. Some feeders are fitted with trays to catch seeds dropped by birds but these are not essential, since any food lost from the feeder is soon found and appreciated by ground-feeding birds, such as pheasants and chaffinches. Large feeders need to be filled no more than once a week, although they are quickly emptied when visited by a flock of finches or sparrows.

Enclosed Feeder
Timid birds may become regular visitors to window feeders. This type of feeder has a roof to keep food dry and high sides to prevent food from spilling out.

Tubular Feeders
Seed feeders ensure a steady flow of seeds for birds, while peanut feeders have a mesh that prevents birds from taking whole peanuts, which may choke their nestlings.

Suction pads for attaching feeder to window

Perch for feeding birds

SEED WINDOW FEEDER

PEANUT WINDOW FEEDER

Log Feeder
This type of feeder is made from a short log with randomly spaced holes bored around the outside. Fat or a birdcake mix can be smeared into the holes. A hook fixed in the top of the feeder allows it to be suspended from a tree or birdtable.

Hanging Feeders
Designed to withstand harsh weather and raids by squirrels, hanging feeders are available as seed or peanut dispensers.

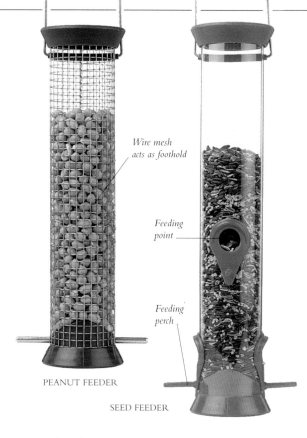

Wire mesh acts as foothold

Feeding point

Feeding perch

PEANUT FEEDER

SEED FEEDER

Hanging feeders can be suspended from trees or birdtables, or mounted on wall brackets. Many of them can be adapted for mounting on stainless-steel poles, which are useful deterrents against squirrels. Convert a hollowed-out log for use as a hanging feeder, by drilling holes on the outside and filling them with birdcake or melted fat. It will be especially popular with visiting woodpeckers, nuthatches, and tits.

Maintaining Feeding Sites
It is a good idea to move feeding sites in the garden regularly, to prevent a build-up of droppings and wasted food. *Salmonella*, which is passed on through droppings, can be transmitted easily to food on birdtables or on the ground. This can be prevented by cleaning birdtables and feeders regularly. Burn any old food and droppings, or wrap them up and put them out for refuse collection. If the disease is suspected to be present, wear protective gloves and thoroughly disinfect birdtables and the ground. Check feeders after heavy rain too, since they can become clogged with wet seed.

Catering for Ground-feeding Birds
Food scattered on lawns or patios will attract birds that are not frequent visitors to birdtables or hanging feeders. Garden visitors might include ducks and long-tailed tits, as well as badgers and hedgehogs. To prevent pheasants and pigeons from plundering food on the ground, place it under a wooden-framed cage made with 5-cm wire netting.

Seed hoppers dispense a steady flow of food for ground-feeding birds and shield the seed from wet weather. The basic patterns for a home-made birdtable and hopper require only simple carpentry skills and can be adapted to suit ground-feeding birds (*see p. 82 and 83*).

Standard Birdtable

Open or covered birdtables can be made from the same basic pattern. The open version is a feeding tray that can be mounted either on short legs for ground-feeding birds or on a tall post. An overhanging roof on the covered model helps to keep food dry. Feeding birds are particularly vulnerable to attack by cats, so choose an open site with an all-round view and protect ground hoppers with wire netting (see p. 86). If a feeder is positioned on your lawn, move it regularly to prevent bare patches from forming.

Cup hooks to suspend birdtable

Hanging feeders can be fixed from feeding tray

Unmounted birdtable can be used as ground feeder

Constructing the Birdtable
Draw outlines of the panels on the wood, then cut them out. Nail each tray side to the base to make an open birdtable. For the roof, nail an upright at a slight outwards slant to each tray corner, then attach the gables. Bevel one side of each roof panel to fit the V-shaped ridge. Screw the ridge into the gables, then nail the roof panels so that they overhang the tray.

Completed Covered Birdtable
This model can be mounted on short legs for use by ground-feeding birds or, with the addition of small, wooden blocks to form a seating underneath the tray, it can be placed on a wooden or galvanized post.

Materials
- 20-mm thick wood for tray
- 9-mm thick plywood for roof
- Rustproof 30-mm nails and screws
- Cup hooks and lengths of chain fitted to ring to suspend; wooden post, four legs, or galvanized pole to mount

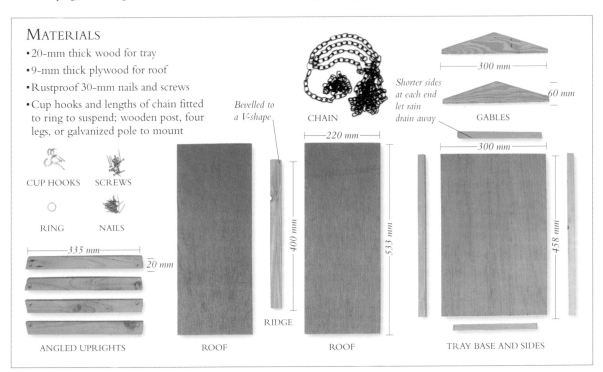

CUP HOOKS   SCREWS

RING   NAILS

335 mm
20 mm

ANGLED UPRIGHTS

Bevelled to a V-shape

ROOF

RIDGE
400 mm

220 mm

ROOF
533 mm

CHAIN

300 mm

Shorter sides at each end let rain drain away

60 mm

GABLES

300 mm

458 mm

TRAY BASE AND SIDES

SEED HOPPER

Seeds can be ruined quickly by wet weather and blown away by strong winds. One practical solution is to use a hopper for dispensing seeds. Small models can be fixed to trees or posts, while larger versions can be placed on open sites for ground-feeding birds.

Constructing the Hopper

Draw pencil outlines of the panels on to the wood, adapting the back panel and base to suit the size of the jar used. Cut out the pieces, then use the long screws to fix the back panel at a right angle to the base. Nail on the sides to form a tray. Leave gaps at each corner of the tray to allow for water drainage. Drill two holes in the base to fit the dowels, which steady the jar, and tack the webbing to the back piece

to secure the jar. Insert three small screws in the base on which the inverted jar can rest. Adjust the gap between the jar rim and the tray to suit the seed size, by turning the screws clockwise or anti-clockwise.

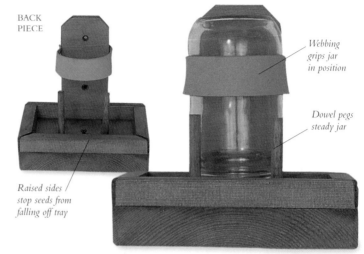

BACK PIECE

Webbing grips jar in position

Dowel pegs steady jar

Raised sides stop seeds from falling off tray

Completed Seed Hopper

Seed hoppers filled with mixed seeds and small fruits can be used to cater for ground-feeding birds such as blackbirds, robins, and chaffinches, which prefer not to hang or perch when they feed.

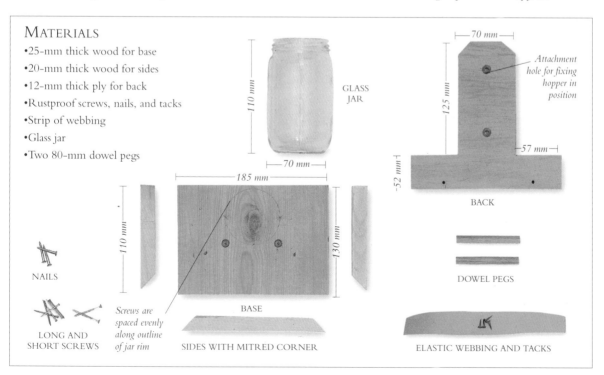

MATERIALS

- 25-mm thick wood for base
- 20-mm thick wood for sides
- 12-mm thick ply for back
- Rustproof screws, nails, and tacks
- Strip of webbing
- Glass jar
- Two 80-mm dowel pegs

110 mm

70 mm

GLASS JAR

70 mm

Attachment hole for fixing hopper in position

125 mm

52 mm

57 mm

BACK

185 mm

110 mm

130 mm

NAILS

LONG AND SHORT SCREWS

Screws are spaced evenly along outline of jar rim

BASE

SIDES WITH MITRED CORNER

DOWEL PEGS

ELASTIC WEBBING AND TACKS

TYPES OF BIRD FOOD

WHOLE
PEANUTS

SHELLED
PEANUTS

WITHIN THE LAST FEW YEARS, birdfeeding
has been transformed beyond simply
putting out stale bread and kitchen scraps,
and perhaps some fat in an old coconut shell,
to providing commercial ready-prepared bird
food, including peanuts, seed mixes, and even
mealworms, which are dispensed in purpose-
made feeders. Some households buy more than
one tonne of bird food every year – a valuable
contribution to helping birds survive.

Peanut Feeders
*Whole peanuts in their shells can
be threaded on a nylon string or
wire. An open-weave net, sealed
at one end and filled with shelled
peanuts, also makes a good feeder.*

Seed Mixtures
A variety of seed mixtures is available, made
up from maize, peanut granules, and sunflower
and other seeds. The strongest rivals to peanuts
are black sunflower seeds, which have thin
skins and soft flesh and are a suitable source of
food for birds when they are feeding nestlings.
Dunnocks, bramblings, and chaffinches favour
pinhead oats, while goldfinches prefer black-
thistle seeds.

RAISINS,
SULTANAS,
AND CURRANTS

Mixed Fruits
*Small, dried fruits can be
added to kitchen scraps or seed
mixtures scattered at feeding
sites or offered on birdtables.*

DRIED
APRICOTS

Fruits and Nuts
Apples and pears, including windfalls, are good
foods for birds in winter, when other natural
sources have finished. Dried fruits, such as
raisins and sultanas, can also be offered, either
added to birdcake or soaked in water. When
scattered on the ground, fruits attract fieldfares,
redwings, blackbirds, and thrushes, as well as
small birds such as tits, blackcaps, and robins.

Rich in fat and very popular with birds, nuts
are a valuable source of energy. Hazelnuts,
almonds, and walnuts can all be put out for
birds, but peanuts are the most common
offering. Always grate peanuts or use wire-
mesh feeders in summer so that whole nuts
are not fed to nestlings. Do not put out salted
peanuts for birds unless they have been

**Sunflower
Feeder**
*A flowerhead may
be hung by its stalk from
a birdtable or post in your garden. Birds will
help themselves to the tightly packed seeds.*

Coconut Feeder
Half a coconut shell threaded with nylon string or wire can be hung upside-down from a birdtable or tree branch. A nesting bird may even use an empty shell as its home.

cake, cooked potatoes, rice, and even cold porridge all make suitable scraps. Make sure that some breadcrumbs and scraps are finely broken up for small, shy birds, like dunnocks.

Some scraps can be hung from a birdtable, perching post, or tree branch. For example, many birds readily feed on hanging strips of cooked meat or bacon rind, provided that they are not too salty, and marrow bones with some meat and fat.

thoroughly washed and dried. Remove any mouldy peanuts from a feeding site, since these contain a toxic substance called aflatoxin. Milky flesh scraped from coconuts is another favourite food that you can offer at birdtables. Alternatively, hang half a coconut shell at a feeding site and let the birds help themselves.

COOKED SPAGHETTI

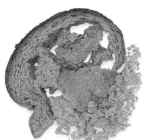

STALE BREAD

Scraps

Kitchen scraps still make a valuable contribution to the birdtable. They attract blackbirds, tits, and robins, as well as larger birds that are greedy and less agile, such as rooks, crows, and starlings. Pre-soaked bread,

Tasty Leftovers
Birds feed on a variety of kitchen scraps. Bread is a useful filler food, while starchy foods like rice and pasta together with fat-rich meat build up reserves of body fat.

BACON RINDS

TYPES OF BIRDCAKE

A good way of presenting nutritious scraps, birdcake can be bought in the form of fat balls, suet sticks, and pudding. To make your own birdcake, melt lard or fat, such as rendered-down fat from cooked meat, and pour it over a mixture of oatmeal, cake, seeds, dried fruits, and scraps, in the ratio of about one-third fat to two-thirds dry mixture. Pour it into a tit-bell or turn out, when cool, on to a birdtable. Do not use polyunsaturated margarine in birdcake.

SEED PUDDING

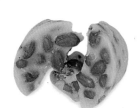

NUT PUDDING

SHREDDED SUET

FAT BALL

SUET STICK

PROTECTING FEEDING SITES

OST GARDEN BIRDS have short lives, and their turnover in numbers is high. It is very distressing to see them meet an abrupt end when they are killed or their nests are robbed by predators. For this reason, try to make sure that your garden encourages birds without increasing the hazards that face them, such as predators and disease.

Keeping Predators at Bay

Cats and foxes are renowned as inveterate and agile hunters of birds and other small creatures. One advantage of a birdtable is that it provides safety in numbers where, together, small birds can keep a constant watch for danger. To protect feeding birds, mount a birdtable or feeder on a galvanized rather than a wooden pole, which is easier to climb, and site it at least 2 m clear of cover from where stealthy climbers may lurk and leap on their prey. A perching post positioned mid-way between a feeding site and cover also offers a useful lookout point.

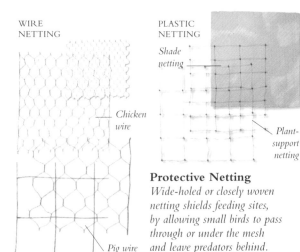

WIRE NETTING

PLASTIC NETTING

Shade netting

Chicken wire

Pig wire

Plant-support netting

Protective Netting
Wide-holed or closely woven netting shields feeding sites, by allowing small birds to pass through or under the mesh and leave predators behind.

Sparrowhawks are natural hunters of small birds and should not be encouraged to visit birdtables. Ornithological studies have found that tits are more likely to escape capture by a sparrowhawk if there is dense growth nearby. In the birdfeeder's garden, birds need a safe haven to which they can escape from predators. This can be provided by conifer or hawthorn hedges, rather than by the sparse foliage of flowerbeds or immature trees.

Deterring Rats

As well as being renowned nest robbers, rats are carriers of *Salmonella*. To deter them from your garden, scatter only sufficient food on the ground for birds to eat during that day.

Beating the Competition

A flock of starlings or just two or three rooks can soon empty a birdtable, taking the food that has been provided for small, shy species. To deter larger species from visiting a feeding site, place food on the ground underneath wire netting with mesh that allows small birds to pass through or squeeze under easily.

Prowling Fox
Foxes are ruthless and agile predators that pose a serious threat to birds during the nesting season. To feed their own young, foxes will take adult birds as well as any nestlings or eggs. Repellants sprinkled around a nest help to prevent fox raids.

Lookout Point
Perching posts are welcomed by birds as lookout points from where they can ensure that the coast is clear of danger. T-shaped rustic poles or similar serve as posts – you may even notice some birds using a garden statue or scarecrow as a watchtower.

Choose a protective feeder if your garden is prone to unwelcome visitors. This type of feeder has built-in defences that deny access to large birds and predators but allow small birds to reach the inner food chamber where they may feed undisturbed. Squirrels are fascinating acrobats to watch in gardens, but they steal food and destroy feeders with their sharp teeth. Commercially available deterrents include a galvanized pole with a tilting metal disc fitted mid-way to prevent squirrels from climbing any further up the pole. One home-made solution is to hang a feeder from a stout wire that has been stretched between two posts or trees. Thread a large plastic bottle on to the wire on each side of the feeder. These baffles spin around when touched, causing squirrels to lose their grip on the wire. Alternatively, suspend the feeder from a very fine wire that squirrels are unable to grasp and walk along.

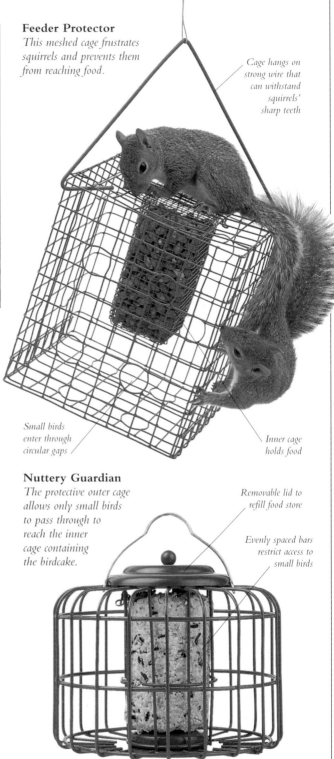

Feeder Protector
This meshed cage frustrates squirrels and prevents them from reaching food.

Cage hangs on strong wire that can withstand squirrels' sharp teeth

Small birds enter through circular gaps

Inner cage holds food

Nuttery Guardian
The protective outer cage allows only small birds to pass through to reach the inner cage containing the birdcake.

Removable lid to refill food store

Evenly spaced bars restrict access to small birds

REGIONAL GUIDE TO PLANTS

EVERY PLANT SPECIES has an ideal environment for growth, but most of the plants described in the catalogue in this chapter are tolerant of a wide range of conditions. The emphasis of the plant catalogue is on native species, including several well-known garden weeds, because exotic plants are sometimes unattractive to birds. Cultivated varieties and related species of common native plants are also recommended in most entries, because they are often better suited to gardens.

The garden environment can often be manipulated to allow a wide variety of plants to flourish, by using simple gardening techniques such as changing the soil acidity or by providing shelter from wind and frost. Not much is known about what birds eat in gardens – especially insect-eating birds – so finding out which plants are favoured by a particular species of bird, either as a source of food or for nesting, presents an interesting challenge for bird gardeners.

Hungry Blackbird
Brightly coloured berries on garden shrubs attract many fruit-eating birds in autumn, and help to supplement their diets.

HOW TO USE THE PLANT CATALOGUE

THIS CHAPTER CONTAINS a catalogue of trees, shrubs, climbers, and herbaceous plants, which have been grouped according to their suitability for a particular region. Each regional section opens with an introduction to the region and a suggested design and planting scheme for a birdfeeder's garden. It also illustrates three bird species that are likely to visit gardens in this region. The plant catalogue for each region comprises individual entries that are organized alphabetically by their botanical names within the plant group. Each entry includes a colour photograph of the plant at maturity and a close-up of the features that are attractive to birds. The accompanying text outlines the appearance and habit of the plant, advises on cultivation, and lists the bird species

that are likely to use the plant. Suggestions are given for related plant species and varieties that are suitable for gardens. At the end of each section is a listing of additional plants that might be included in your garden.

Planting Guide
Finding different species of plant that attract visitors to your bird garden can be a rewarding project. When choosing plants for your garden consider local conditions, such as soil type, exposure to wind and sun, and the effect of air pollution – this includes smoke and chemicals as well as salt-laden air on the coast. Most of the plants listed are native to certain parts of Europe, but many of them are tolerant of a broad range of conditions.

GUIDE TO EACH REGIONAL SECTION

CENTRAL REGION
Identified by pale green border

NORTHERN REGION
Identified by pale blue border

SOUTHERN REGION
Identified by pale orange border

WHAT TO PLANT
Outlines range of plants used in planting scheme

PLANTING LIST
Lists plants shown in regional garden scheme

LOCATOR MAP
Indicates extent of region

INTRODUCTION
Describes main characteristics of region and any special gardening needs

GARDEN ILLUSTRATION
Shows suggested planting scheme and layout for regional garden

GARDEN FEATURE
Highlights special features in garden

BIRD ILLUSTRATION
Shows bird species that is likely to visit region

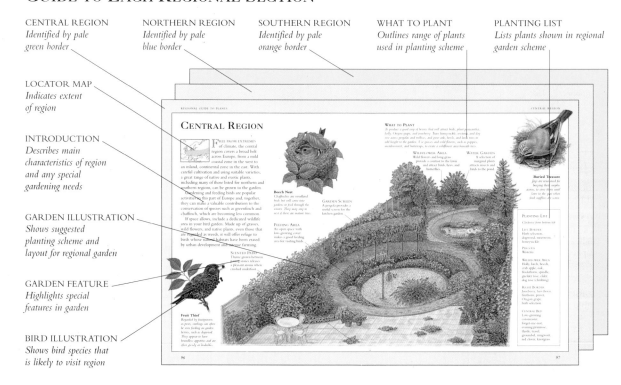

GUIDE TO REGIONAL PLANT CATALOGUE

PLANT GROUP
Identifies plant category

COMMON NAME
Non-scientific name by which plant is known

PLANT PROFILE
Describes native habitat and flowering and fruiting habit

CULTIVATION
Advises on preferred growing conditions and routine care of plant

PLANT DETAIL
Highlights feature(s) that attract birds

BIRD USE
Lists bird species that are attracted to plant

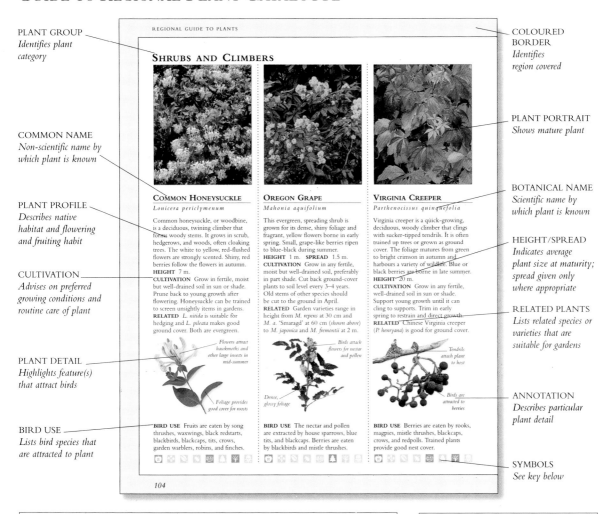

REGIONAL GUIDE TO PLANTS

SHRUBS AND CLIMBERS

COMMON HONEYSUCKLE
Lonicera periclymenum

Common honeysuckle, or woodbine, is a deciduous, twining climber that forms woody stems. It grows in scrub, hedgerows, and woods, often cloaking trees. The white to yellow, red-flushed flowers are strongly scented. Shiny, red berries follow the flowers in autumn.
HEIGHT 7 m.
CULTIVATION Grow in fertile, moist but well-drained soil in sun or shade. Prune back to young growth after flowering. Honeysuckle can be trained to screen unsightly items in gardens.
RELATED *L. nitida* is suitable for hedging and *L. pileata* makes good ground cover. Both are evergreen.

Flowers attract hawkmoths and other large insects in mid-summer

Foliage provides good cover for roosts

BIRD USE Fruits are eaten by song thrushes, waxwings, black redstarts, blackbirds, blackcaps, tits, crows, garden warblers, robins, and finches.

OREGON GRAPE
Mahonia aquifolium

This evergreen, spreading shrub is grown for its dense, shiny foliage and fragrant, yellow flowers borne in early spring. Small, grape-like berries ripen to blue-black during summer.
HEIGHT 1 m. **SPREAD** 1.5 m.
CULTIVATION Grow in any fertile, moist but well-drained soil, preferably in part shade. Cut back ground-cover plants to soil level every 3–4 years. Old stems of other species should be cut to the ground in April.
RELATED Garden varieties range in height from *M. repens* at 30 cm and *M. a.* 'Smaragd' at 60 cm (*shown above*) to *M. japonica* and *M. fremontii* at 2 m.

Birds attack flowers for nectar and pollen

Dense, glossy foliage

BIRD USE The nectar and pollen are extracted by house sparrows, blue tits, and blackcaps. Berries are eaten by blackbirds and mistle thrushes.

VIRGINIA CREEPER
Parthenocissus quinquefolia

Virginia creeper is a quick-growing, deciduous, woody climber that clings with sucker-tipped tendrils. It is often trained up trees or grown as ground cover. The foliage matures from green to bright crimson in autumn and harbours a variety of wildlife. Blue or black berries are borne in late summer.
HEIGHT 20 m.
CULTIVATION Grow in any fertile, well-drained soil in sun or shade. Support young growth until it can cling to supports. Trim in early spring to restrain and direct growth.
RELATED Chinese Virginia creeper (*P. henryana*) is good for ground cover.

Tendrils attach plant to host

Birds are attracted to berries

BIRD USE Berries are eaten by rooks, magpies, mistle thrushes, blackcaps, crows, and redpolls. Trained plants provide good nest cover.

104

COLOURED BORDER
Identifies region covered

PLANT PORTRAIT
Shows mature plant

BOTANICAL NAME
Scientific name by which plant is known

HEIGHT/SPREAD
Indicates average plant size at maturity; spread given only where appropriate

RELATED PLANTS
Lists related species or varieties that are suitable for gardens

ANNOTATION
Describes particular plant detail

SYMBOLS
See key below

HOW PLANTS ARE NAMED

All plants are named according to an internationally recognized hierarchy of botanical categories. The most commonly used divisions are:

GENUS/SPECIES *Euonymus fortunei*
The first Latin name (*Euonymus*) indicates the plant's genus, which is applied to single or a number of closely related species. The second Latin name (*fortunei*) identifies the individual species.

SUBSPECIES *Euonymus hamiltonianus* subsp. *sieboldianus* (syn. *E. yedoensis*)
A subspecies is a major division within an individual species. Synonyms (syn.) are botanical names that have been superseded following reclassification.

VARIETY *Euonymus fortunei* var. *radicans*
A variety has minor variations of an individual species or subspecies. It is sometimes shown as form (f.).

CULTIVAR *Euonymus fortunei* 'Kewensis'
A cultivated variety is raised artificially for uniform features and stability that can be maintained by propagation.

HYBRID *Euonymus* x *hamiltonianus*
A hybrid is artificially or naturally cross-bred from two species.

KEY TO SYMBOLS

These identify key plant features that attract birds and are shown in orange. "Toxic" warns that all or some of the plant's parts are toxic.

Fruits   Nest cover

Seeds   Evergreen

Leaves   Deciduous

Insects   Toxic

GARDENING THROUGHOUT THE YEAR

EVERY SEASON has a set of specific tasks that need to be carried out in the bird garden. The tasks listed below are not exclusive and are intended only as a guide. They may be carried out earlier or later in the year, depending on the region where you live. As you become more familiar with your garden and the habits of visiting birds, you can compile your own log of seasonal tasks and observations.

Autumn

This is the time to prepare the garden for the following year and to welcome back winter populations of immigrant and native birds.
- Collect or buy seeds for planting.
- Plant or transplant any shrubs or trees.
- Leave the dead stems of herbaceous plants so that insects have a safe place to overwinter.
- Cover the pond with netting until all deciduous leaves have been shed.
- Rake up dead leaves for composting.

- Put up new nestboxes. Clean out existing nestboxes by removing old nest material.
- Refurbish birdtables and feeders, and stock up with fresh supplies of seeds and nuts.

Winter

This is a quiet time of year for the gardener, but a busy period for the birdfeeder's garden. Birds will visit regularly, attracted by birdtables, scattered scraps and seeds, and well-stocked peanut feeders. Look out for unusual species that may be drawn into your garden during severe weather. Towards the end of winter, courtship and nesting behaviour can be seen and early breeders will start to lay.
- Plant and mulch when the weather permits.
- Prune apple trees.
- Check birdbaths and ponds regularly to remove any ice. Keep the water topped up.
- Dig over any heavy soil. Frosts will break it down and birds will enjoy the exposed pests.

Autumn Harvest
In autumn, poppies produce large quantities of seeds held inside "pepperpot" capsules.

Winter Haven
Tall grasses and seedheads should be left in the garden in winter to provide shelter and food for birds.

Summer Climbers
Tall and climbing plants should be supported with canes in summer or trained against a trellis or wire.

Pond Care in Spring
Leaf litter and algae need to be removed in spring, and any root-bound aquatic plants should be repotted.

Spring

This is a busy time of year for gardeners and birds alike. Birds are most vulnerable in spring, when their natural food supplies have run low.

- Continue putting out food in the nesting season because the garden may not provide enough to cater for hungry nestlings.
- Put up any remaining nestboxes.
- Clear away any annuals and tidy herbaceous shrubs from the previous season.
- Prepare beds for planting by digging over, weeding, and mulching.
- Plant and sow seeds once the ground shows signs of warming up.
- Feed and mulch established plants.
- Sweep away winter debris from the lawn. For the lawn's first cut of the year, set the mower blade at its highest position.

Summer

This is the best time to watch birds nesting, but take care not to disturb them when gardening. As nesting finishes and the birds disperse, look out for early migrant warblers, which may spend a few days in the garden.

- Plant annuals and winter salad vegetables.
- Water new plants regularly.
- Mow grass lightly when lawns are very dry.
- Keep weeds under control and dead-head plants unless they produce seeds or berries.
- Stake and tie up tall perennials.
- Feed plants in hanging baskets and pots.
- Provide extra food for birds in dry weather.
- Keep the birdbath and pond topped up.
- Harvest any fruits or vegetables that are intended for you, rather than for the birds. Protect any prized specimens with netting.

THE CLIMATE

WHEN PLANNING YOUR GARDEN, the effect of climate is an important consideration that influences the success of your planting scheme and your choice of plants. The length of the growing season, for example, is determined by the local climate and the latitude of the region because it depends on air temperature and daylight hours. While plants grow best in conditions that closely match their native habitats, some are able to adapt to different climates. Less hardy or even exotic species can be grown successfully if nurtured carefully. Many of them need to be watered regularly in dry regions, and they will need to be shielded from wind, frost, and snow.

The climate in which you live affects the bird species seen in your garden because of its influence on their food supply. Many small birds, such as swallows, swifts, flycatchers, and warblers, migrate south for the winter when insects become scarce. A few species can stay on their home territories by changing their diets. Seed- and fruit-eaters are able to cope with cold winters but they have to migrate in years when crops are poor due to bad weather.

TEMPERATURE AND RAINFALL

AVERAGE MINIMUM TEMPERATURE (°C)	AVERAGE ANNUAL RAINFALL (cm)
4–6°C	0–25 cm
0–4°C	25–50 cm
⁻5–0°C	50–75 cm
⁻10–⁻5°C	75–100 cm
⁻15–⁻10°C	100–150 cm
>⁻15°C	150–250 cm

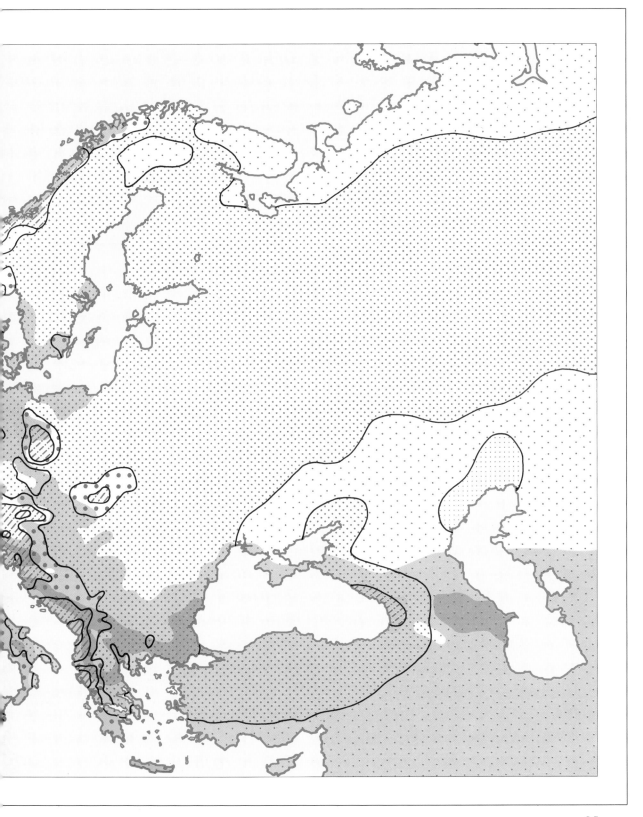

CENTRAL REGION

FREE FROM EXTREMES of climate, the central region covers a broad belt across Europe, from a mild coastal zone in the west to an inland, continental zone in the east. With careful cultivation and using suitable varieties, a great range of native and exotic plants, including many of those listed for northern and southern regions, can be grown in the garden.

Gardening and feeding birds are popular activities in this part of Europe. Together, they can help towards the conservation of greenfinches, chaffinches, and other species whose numbers need to be encouraged.

If space allows, include a dedicated wildlife area in your bird garden. Made up of grasses, wild flowers, and native plants, even those that are regarded as weeds, it will offer refuge to birds whose natural habitats have been erased by urban development and intensive farming.

Beech Nest
Chaffinches are woodland birds but will come into gardens to feed through the winter. They may stay to nest if there are mature trees.

GARDEN SCREEN
A pergola provides a useful screen for the kitchen garden.

FEEDING AREA
An open space with low-growing cover makes a good feeding area for visiting birds.

SCENTED PATIO
Thyme grown between paving stones releases a pleasant aroma when crushed underfoot.

Fruit Thief
Regarded by fruitgrowers as pests, starlings can often be seen feeding on garden berries, such as dogwood. They appear to have boundless appetites and are often greedy at birdtables.

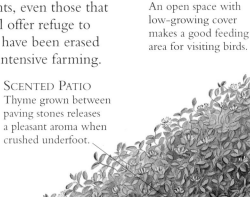

WHAT TO PLANT

To produce a good crop of berries that will attract birds, plant pyracantha, holly, Oregon grape, and juneberry. Train honeysuckle, wisteria, and dog rose across pergolas and trellises, and grow oak, beech, and larch trees to add height to the garden. Use grasses and wild flowers, such as poppies, meadowsweet, and buttercups, to create a wildflower area beneath trees.

WILDFLOWER AREA

Wild flowers and long grass provide a contrast to the lawn and attract birds, bees, and butterflies.

WATER GARDEN

A selection of marginal plants attracts insects and birds to the pond.

Buried Treasure
Jays are renowned for burying their surplus acorns, to store them until later in the year when food supplies are scarce.

PLANTING LIST

Clockwise from bottom left

LEFT BORDER
Herb selection, dogwood, mezereon, honeysuckle

PERGOLA
Wisteria

WILDFLOWER AREA
Holly, larch, beech, crab apple, oak, blackthorn, spindle, guelder rose, elder, dog rose (climbing)

RIGHT BORDER
Juneberry, hawthorn, firethorn, privet, Oregon grape, herb selection

CENTRAL BED
Low-growing cotoneaster, forget-me-not, evening primrose, thistle, teasel, groundsel, mugwort, red clover, knotgrass

TREES

SYCAMORE

Acer pseudoplatanus

The fast-growing sycamore thrives in towns and on exposed coastal sites. It is commonly used as an ornamental feature in gardens but also makes an effective windbreak when planted in rows on open sites. Sycamore is valued in wildlife gardens because its foliage supports large numbers of insects.
HEIGHT 30 m. **SPREAD** 15 m.
CULTIVATION Grow in fertile, moist but well-drained soil in sun or part shade. Transplant young trees between October and March.
RELATED *A. p.* 'Atropurpureum' and *A. p. f. erythrocarpum* both produce red-winged fruit.

Sycamore leaves are good source of aphids

Winged seeds sprout vigorously and may be invasive

BIRD USE Seeds are eaten by tits, waxwings, jays, chaffinches, and bramblings. Many birds are attracted to aphids found on the leaves.

COMMON HAWTHORN

Crataegus monogyna

The common hawthorn is a small, deciduous tree with spiny twigs, which grows in hedgerows, woods, and scrub. It is valued for its long season of interest and tolerance of polluted or exposed sites. Round, red berries, or haws, ripen in September. They last throughout winter but are prone to damage during cold weather.
HEIGHT 10 m. **SPREAD** 8 m.
CULTIVATION Grow in any soil in sun or part shade. Trim hedges with care after flowering, since the fruits are borne only on old shoots.
RELATED *C. laevigata* (*shown above*) is useful for hedging in gardens.

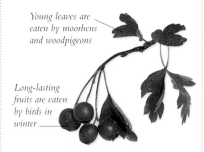

Young leaves are eaten by moorhens and woodpigeons

Long-lasting fruits are eaten by birds in winter

BIRD USE Fruits are eaten by black redstarts, pheasants, waxwings, crows, starlings, finches, blue tits, thrushes, and blackcaps.

LEYLAND CYPRESS

x Cupressocyparis leylandii

This fast-growing, evergreen conifer is widely used in gardens as a hedge, screen, or windbreak. Leyland cypress supports a surprising amount of wildlife in its dense sprays of foliage.
HEIGHT 35 m. **SPREAD** 5 m.
CULTIVATION Plant 75 cm apart in deep, well-drained soil in sun or part shade. Trim the tops to the desired height, but avoid excessive trimming so as not to disturb resident wildlife.
RELATED x *C. l.* 'Haggerston Grey' (*shown above*) has grey-green foliage; x *C. l.* 'Castlewellan Gold' has golden foliage. Grow several cultivars together to produce a contrasting hedge.

Dense foliage provides good cover for nests

Some birds extract seeds from cones

BIRD USE Tits, goldcrests, and dunnocks feed on the small, resident insects. Coal tits, blue tits, siskins, and other finches eat the cone seeds.

SPINDLE TREE

Euonymus europaeus

Spindle is a small, deciduous shrub or tree that is grown in gardens for its pink fruits and attractive autumn foliage. Clusters of greenish-white flowers appear in June, with male and female flowers often borne on different trees. The fruits split open in autumn to reveal their seeds.

HEIGHT 6 m. **SPREAD** 2 m.
CULTIVATION Grow in preferably limestone soil in sun or part shade.
RELATED *E. fortunei* var. *radicans* is a creeper that provides good ground cover. The evergreen Japanese spindle (*E. japonicus*) is useful for hedging and tolerates air pollution and salt spray.

COMMON BEECH

Fagus sylvatica

The large, graceful beech tree is widely grown as an ornamental in parks or as hedging in gardens. Tassel-like male catkins appear after the leaves in groups of two or three. The female catkins develop into bristly husks containing small, edible nuts known as mast. In good years, large numbers of seeds are produced.

HEIGHT 30 m. **SPREAD** 25 m.
CULTIVATION Grow in well-drained, preferably chalky soil in full sun or part shade. Trees that are less than 2.5 m high keep their leaves in winter.
RELATED Copper beech (*F. s. var. purpurea*) has purple-brown leaves.

COMMON HOLLY

Ilex aquifolium

Common holly is a small, evergreen tree or shrub found in hedgerows and woods. It is tolerant of polluted sites and salt spray. Individual trees are either male or female. The female plant produces clusters of red or yellow berries only if a male plant is growing nearby to provide pollen.

HEIGHT 3–15 m. **SPREAD** 5 m.
CULTIVATION Grow in moist but well-drained, fertile soil in sun or shade. Trim young plants into shape.
RELATED *I. a.* 'J. C. Van Tol' produces a good crop of berries without pollination and is suitable for growing in a container.

Birds are attracted to brightly coloured berries

Leaves are host to aphids and caterpillars

Thick foliage makes good nesting material

Waxwings eat leaf buds

Stiff leaves shield birds from predators and harsh weather

Berries are valuable source of winter food

BIRD USE Fruits are eaten by thrushes, woodpigeons, starlings, tits, sparrows, blackcaps, garden warblers, waxwings, crows, bramblings, and other finches.

BIRD USE Nuts are eaten by siskins, nuthatches, ring-necked parakeets, tits, crows, great spotted woodpeckers, crossbills, and bramblings.

BIRD USE Berries are eaten by robins, waxwings, blackcaps, woodpigeons, bullfinches, and thrushes. Many birds nest or shelter in the dense foliage.

TREES

EUROPEAN LARCH

Larix decidua

European larch is a deciduous conifer that is tolerant of a wide range of conditions. It bears tiny flowers in spring, followed by soft needles that turn from green to orange in autumn. Upright, brown cones, which develop from the female flowers, shed seeds in autumn to be dispersed on the wind.
HEIGHT 50 m. **SPREAD** 5–15 m.
CULTIVATION Grow in deep, well-drained soil in full sun, but avoid wet soil and dry, shallow chalk.
RELATED Fast-growing and disease-free Japanese larch (*L. kaempferi*) and hybrid larch (*L. x marschlinsii*) are more commonly grown varieties.

Dispersed cone seeds can be enjoyed by ground-feeding birds

Crossbills prise open cones to extract seeds

BIRD USE Seeds are eaten by great spotted woodpeckers, marsh tits, coal tits, nuthatches, bramblings, serins, siskins, crossbills, and other finches.

COMMON CRAB APPLE

Malus sylvestris

The common crab apple is the ancestor of cultivated apples. It grows wild in woods and hedgerows and is tolerant of most soils. Its compact, bushy growth makes it suitable for growing in small gardens. The white blossom, often tinged pink, is borne in late April, followed by small, greenish apples, or pomes, with dry, sour flesh.
HEIGHT 10 m. **SPREAD** 10 m.
CULTIVATION Grow in any well-drained soil in full sun, although part shade is tolerated. Prune in winter.
RELATED *M.* 'Red Sentinel' (*shown above*) and the Siberian crab apple (*M. baccata*) bear long-lasting fruits.

Birds are attracted to leaves, which harbour caterpillars

Fruits have sour taste

BIRD USE Pheasants, moorhens, green woodpeckers, blackcaps, waxwings, thrushes, and crows eat the fruits. Tits, finches, and blackcaps enjoy the seeds.

BLACKTHORN

Prunus spinosa

The blackthorn is a deciduous, spiny shrub or tree that is usually found growing in hedgerows and woods. Its suckers form dense thickets around the base of the tree when left unchecked. The round, shiny, black fruits, or sloes, contain large stones and have a dry, bitter taste. They ripen in September and remain on the tree through winter.
HEIGHT 4 m. **SPREAD** 3 m.
CULTIVATION Grow in any moist but well-drained soil in full sun. Trim after flowering, and remove suckers.
RELATED *P. s.* 'Purpurea' (*shown above*) bears red leaves that mature to deep crimson-purple.

Dark, shiny fruits are valuable source of food in winter

Crossbills eat stones found inside sloes

BIRD USE Pheasants, woodpigeons, waxwings, thrushes, starlings, and crows eat the fruits. The stones are sometimes eaten by tits and finches.

COMMON OAK

Quercus robur

The common oak is a slow-growing, deciduous tree that is found in woods, hedgerows, and parks. It is not suitable for growing in small gardens. Dark green leaves appear in May, followed by a second growth of shoots in July or August. Male catkins appear in May, together with the female flowers borne on stalks. Acorns develop from the flowers and fall in autumn. Oak trees host more insect types than any other species of European tree.
HEIGHT 30–40 m. **SPREAD** 25 m.
CULTIVATION Plant in deep soil.
RELATED *Q. r.* 'Concordia' grows to a height and spread of 10 m.

Acorns attract many garden birds

Flowers and leaves emerge together

BIRD USE Acorns attract finches, tits, woodpeckers, nuthatches, pheasants, and pigeons. Woodpigeons, mistle thrushes, and crows nest in oak trees.

GOAT WILLOW

Salix caprea

Goat willow is a small, fast-growing, deciduous tree, grown for its catkins and foliage. It is commonly found in woods and often colonizes waste ground. The silver (female) and yellow (male) catkins are borne on separate trees in spring, before the foliage.
HEIGHT 10 m. **SPREAD** 8 m.
CULTIVATION Grow in any deep soil in full sun. Goat willow dislikes chalk but thrives in dry soil. Site away from drains because roots can be invasive.
RELATED *S. c.* 'Kilmarnock' is a small, "weeping" variety. Grey willow (*S. cinerea*) is smaller and bushier. *S. lindleyana* is low and spreading.

Buds are stripped by birds

Blue tits and blackcaps drink nectar from catkins

BIRD USE Waxwings, marsh tits, and coal tits eat the flowers and buds. Seeds are eaten by chaffinches, greenfinches, siskins, bullfinches, and hawfinches.

COMMON ELDER

Sambucus nigra

Common elder is a deciduous shrub or small tree that grows in woodlands and thickets. It forms a colony easily but can be a nuisance in gardens when self-sown plants become dominant. The scented, creamy-white blossom borne in June is pollinated by small flies, which attract insect-eating birds.
HEIGHT 4 m. **SPREAD** 4 m.
CULTIVATION Grow in moist, fertile soil in sun. Prune old shoots in winter and remove unwanted seedlings.
RELATED *S. n.* 'Aurea' is a very hardy cultivar with attractive golden-yellow foliage. Red-berried elder (*S. racemosa*) is smaller and bushy.

Birds are attracted to glossy, black berries

Upright berries tip downwards when ripe

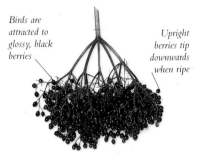

BIRD USE Berries attract finches, ring-necked parakeets, crows, thrushes, spotted flycatchers, starlings, moorhens, waxwings, and garden warblers.

SHRUBS AND CLIMBERS

JUNEBERRY

Amelanchier lamarckii

The juneberry is a deciduous shrub or small tree grown for its mass of white, star-shaped flowers in late spring. Its bronze foliage matures through dark green to red and orange in autumn. Green berries ripen to sweet, juicy, purple-black fruits in summer and are popular with birds.
HEIGHT 6 m. **SPREAD** 3 m.
CULTIVATION Grow in well-drained or moist soil that is moderately acid, in full sun or part shade. Prune during winter to keep plant shape.
RELATED *A. arborea, A. laevis,* and *A. canadensis* are similar species that are often confused with *A. lamarckii.*

Pollinating insects on flowers attract birds

Leaves unfold with flowers

BIRD USE Berries are eaten by crows, waxwings, redstarts, starlings, garden warblers, thrushes, magpies, blackcaps, jays, chaffinches, and greenfinches.

COMMON DOGWOOD

Cornus sanguinea

Dogwood is a deciduous bush or small tree that grows on chalky soil. It is commonly found in hedgerows, woods, and scrub. The red shoots present a colourful display in gardens in winter. Dense clusters of white flowers are borne in summer, followed by small, round berries, which ripen from green to dull blue-black.
HEIGHT 4 m. **SPREAD** 3 m.
CULTIVATION Grow in fertile, chalky soil in full sun. Dogwood will grow from suckers and colonizes easily.
RELATED *C. canadensis* grows in acid soil and is suitable for woodland gardens or for use as ground cover.

Many birds are attracted to berries

Small berries are easy for birds to eat

BIRD USE Berries are eaten by spotted flycatchers, thrushes, garden warblers, woodpeckers, tits, waxwings, crows, blackcaps, and finches.

COTONEASTER

Cotoneaster microphyllus

Cotoneaster is an evergreen shrub with rigid, often drooping branches, and glossy, dark green leaves. Small, white flowers appear from late spring to summer, followed by red fruits.
HEIGHT 1 m. **SPREAD** 2 m.
CULTIVATION Grow in moderately well-drained soil in sun or part shade. Extend the fruiting season by planting a selection of species.
RELATED Prostrate *C. horizontalis* suits walls, banks, and ground cover, especially in small gardens. *C. dammeri* is ideal for banks and ground cover beneath other shrubs. *C. bullatus* fruits early and *C. distychus* is late-fruiting.

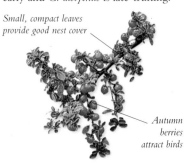

Small, compact leaves provide good nest cover

Autumn berries attract birds

BIRD USE Berries are eaten by jays, thrushes, ring-necked parakeets, starlings, blackcaps, tree sparrows, finches, and waxwings.

MEZEREON

Daphne mezereum

Mezereon is a small, deciduous shrub that grows on limestone soils. It is a common sight in woodlands, rock gardens, and shrub borders. Its fragrant, pink to purplish-pink flowers make a striking display in late winter and early spring, before the leathery, green leaves emerge. Fleshy, red fruits ripen in May and June.
HEIGHT 1 m. **SPREAD** 1 m.
CULTIVATION Grow in moderately fertile, well-drained soil in full sun. Mulch regularly to keep roots cool. Keep pruning to a minimum.
RELATED *D. m.* 'Alba' bears white flowers and amber fruits.

Aphids on leaves attract birds

Fleshy fruits are enjoyed by garden birds

BIRD USE Fruits are eaten by thrushes, waxwings, black redstarts, starlings, tits, spotted flycatchers, crows, warblers, and finches. Blackcaps drink nectar.

COMMON IVY

Hedera helix

This evergreen climber with woody stems can usually be found growing in woods and hedgerows. It is tolerant of air pollution. Ivy clings firmly to trees or walls by means of small, clinging tendrils and can also spread rapidly over ground. Yellow-green flowers open from September to November, while the berries ripen from January through to spring.
HEIGHT 10 m. **SPREAD** 5 m.
CULTIVATION Grow in well-drained soil. Tolerates shade but will only flower in the sun. Avoid trimming.
RELATED *H. h.* 'Cavendishii' is excellent for growing against a wall.

Berries are valuable winter food for birds

Foliage makes good year-round cover for roosts

BIRD USE Berries are eaten by jays, collared doves, black redstarts, thrushes, starlings, waxwings, blackcaps, woodpigeons, and finches.

COMMON PRIVET

Ligustrum vulgare

Privet is a fast-growing, deciduous shrub that is commonly found in hedgerows and scrub. It is ideal for garden hedging. Scented, white flowers open in early to mid-summer, followed by ripe, black berries.
HEIGHT 5 m. **SPREAD** 3 m.
CULTIVATION Grow in well-drained soil, preferably limestone, in sun. Cut back to 30 cm after planting and trim in summer. Hard cutting improves its value as cover for nests, but leave plant untrimmed for flowering and fruiting.
RELATED Japanese privet (*L. japonicum*) and golden privet (*L. ovalifolium* 'Aureum') suit hedging.

Berries remain on bush throughout winter

Dense foliage provides good nesting cover

BIRD USE Berries are eaten by jays, waxwings, redstarts, tits, blackbirds, nuthatches, magpies, blackcaps, robins, woodpigeons, warblers, and finches.

SHRUBS AND CLIMBERS

COMMON HONEYSUCKLE

Lonicera periclymenum

Common honeysuckle, or woodbine, is a deciduous, twining climber that forms woody stems. It grows in scrub, hedgerows, and woods, often cloaking trees. The white to yellow, red-flushed flowers are strongly scented. Shiny, red berries follow the flowers in autumn.
HEIGHT 7 m.
CULTIVATION Grow in fertile, moist but well-drained soil in sun or shade. Prune back to young growth after flowering. Honeysuckle can be trained to screen unsightly items in gardens.
RELATED *L. nitida* is suitable for hedging and *L. pileata* makes good ground cover. Both are evergreen.

Flowers attract hawkmoths and other large insects in mid-summer

Foliage provides good cover for roosts

BIRD USE Fruits are eaten by song thrushes, waxwings, black redstarts, blackbirds, blackcaps, tits, crows, garden warblers, robins, and finches.

OREGON GRAPE

Mahonia aquifolium

This evergreen, spreading shrub is grown for its dense, shiny foliage and fragrant, yellow flowers borne in early spring. Small, grape-like berries ripen to blue-black during summer.
HEIGHT 1 m. **SPREAD** 1.5 m.
CULTIVATION Grow in any fertile, moist but well-drained soil, preferably in part shade. Cut back ground-cover plants to soil level every 3–4 years. Old stems of other species should be cut to the ground in April.
RELATED Garden varieties range in height from *M. repens* at 30 cm and *M. a.* 'Smaragd' at 60 cm (*shown above*) to *M. japonica* and *M. fremontii* at 2 m.

Birds attack flowers for nectar and pollen

Dense, glossy foliage

BIRD USE The nectar and pollen are extracted by house sparrows, blue tits, and blackcaps. Berries are eaten by blackbirds and mistle thrushes.

VIRGINIA CREEPER

Parthenocissus quinquefolia

Virginia creeper is a quick-growing, deciduous, woody climber that clings with sucker-tipped tendrils. It is often trained up trees or grown as ground cover. The foliage matures from green to bright crimson in autumn and harbours a variety of wildlife. Blue or black berries are borne in late summer.
HEIGHT 20 m.
CULTIVATION Grow in any fertile, well-drained soil in sun or shade. Support young growth until it can cling to supports. Trim in early spring to restrain and direct growth.
RELATED Chinese Virginia creeper (*P. henryana*) is good for ground cover.

Tendrils attach plant to host

Birds are attracted to berries

BIRD USE Berries are eaten by rooks, magpies, mistle thrushes, blackcaps, crows, and redpolls. Trained plants provide good nest cover.

DOG ROSE

Rosa canina

Dog rose is a deciduous, climbing shrub that grows in woods, scrub, and hedgerows. Its thorns help to anchor the stems to neighbouring plants or to each other. The pink or white flowers open in June, followed by fleshy, red fruits, or hips, which ripen in September. The seed-laden hips remain juicy until the end of winter, when they shrivel and blacken.
HEIGHT 3 m.
CULTIVATION Grow in fertile soil in sun. Trim to shape in winter, then prune in February to allow fruiting.
RELATED Field rose (*R. arvensis*) grows to 1 m high.

Blackbirds and song thrushes nest in thick growth

Hips are packed with tiny seeds

House sparrows and blue tits eat aphids on leaves

BIRD USE Hips are eaten by thrushes, woodpigeons, waxwings, tits, jays, magpies, rooks, blackcaps, garden warblers, serins, and other finches.

GUELDER ROSE

Viburnum opulus

Guelder rose is a deciduous shrub or small tree that grows in damp woods, hedgerows, and scrub. Clusters of white flowers in spring are followed by bright red berries, which remain on the plant after the leaves have fallen.
HEIGHT 4 m. **SPREAD** 4 m.
CULTIVATION Grow in moderately fertile, moist but well-drained soil, in full sun or part shade.
RELATED *V. o.* 'Compactum' (*shown above*) is slow-growing and dense. Laurustinus (*V. tinus*) is evergreen and tolerates salt and shade. The wayfaring tree (*V. lantana*) bears red fruits, which ripen to black, and suits gardens.

Foliage hosts aphids and whitefly

Ripe, scarlet berries attract garden birds

BIRD USE Berries are eaten by jays, bramblings, blackcaps, thrushes, marsh tits, waxwings, collared doves, garden warblers, bullfinches, and hawfinches.

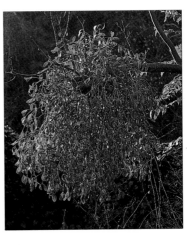

MISTLETOE

Viscum album

This evergreen, semi-parasitic plant grows in rounded masses on deciduous trees. It is commonly found on apple, hawthorn, lime, and poplar trees, where the seed has germinated and sent a root into the tissue of the host plant to draw water and nutrients. Tiny green flowers open from February to April. The white berries ripen in November and December.
HEIGHT 1 m. **SPREAD** 1 m.
CULTIVATION Make a small cut in the bark of a host tree during spring and smear a berry across the cut to fill it with seed. Secure with a loop of raffia to ensure successful germination.

Distinctive paired leaves

Birds spread seeds by wiping their bills against other trees

BIRD USE Berries are eaten by mistle thrushes, song thrushes, house and tree sparrows, blackbirds, robins, redwings, blackcaps, and waxwings.

HERBACEOUS PLANTS

MUGWORT

Artemisia vulgaris

Mugwort is a perennial herb that is generally regarded as a weed. It grows on waste land, roadsides, and in hedgerows, and suits rock gardens and borders. It is easily recognized by its green, aromatic, fern-like leaves with silvery undersides. Small, rust-brown flowers are borne in mid- to late summer, followed by seeds in autumn.
HEIGHT 1.2 m. **SPREAD** 1 m.
CULTIVATION Grow in well-drained, fertile soil in full sun. Mugwort seeds freely, but can also be increased by cuttings taken in late spring.
RELATED Tarragon (*A. dracunculus*) is useful for a herb or kitchen garden.

Clusters of tiny seeds are eaten by many garden birds

BIRD USE The autumn seeds are eaten by reed buntings, serins, greenfinches, siskins, goldfinches, and linnets. Drifts of mugwort provide ground cover.

WILD CABBAGE

Brassica oleracea

The wild cabbage is a tall biennial or perennial with a woody base and large, lobed leaves. It is commonly found growing on sea cliffs, rocky slopes, and waste ground. White flowers are borne in summer. Cultivated cabbages, including cauliflower, broccoli, and kale, are grown as annuals, while some cultivars are grown as ornamentals.
HEIGHT AND SPREAD 30–45 cm.
CULTIVATION Sow under glass in January or in a seedbed in April. Plant out in June. Take care not to damage the roots, which lie near the surface.
RELATED Turnip, rape, and mustard are close wild relatives.

Long, pointed seeds appear after flowers

Flowerheads of "bolted" cabbages attract insects

BIRD USE Seeds are eaten by woodpigeons, collared doves, marsh tits, house sparrows, bramblings, serins, greenfinches, and linnets.

WELTED THISTLE

Carduus acanthoides

The welted thistle is a biennial that is usually found on waste land, verges, and in hedgerows. Its purple flowers open from June to August, followed by ripe seeds in September. Although thistles are regarded as weeds, several species are cultivated for their flowerheads and foliage, and are ideal at the backs of flower borders.
HEIGHT 1.2 m. **SPREAD** 50 cm.
CULTIVATION Sow seeds in May, either *in situ* or in a nursery bed, and transfer in September. Self-seeds freely and may become invasive.
RELATED Nodding or musk thistle (*C. nutans*) has red-purple flowers.

Spiny tips protect flowerhead

Many insects are attracted to flowers

Leaves are edged with sharp spines

BIRD USE Autumn thistle seeds are eaten by marsh tits, siskins, dunnocks, linnets, greenfinches, goldfinches, and crossbills.

TEASEL

Dipsacus fullonum

Teasel is a biennial or short-lived perennial herb that grows on rough banks, pasture land, and roadsides. It bears a rosette of large leaves and, in the second year, a prickly stem topped with heads of tiny, purple flowers. The seedheads are ideal as winter display in the garden, or for indoor decoration.
HEIGHT 2 m. **SPREAD** 60 cm.
CULTIVATION Grow in any moderately fertile soil, including heavy clay, in sun or part shade.
RELATED Fuller's teasel (*D. f.* subsp. *sativus, shown below, right*), is grown for its stiff seedheads, which were once used for raising the nap of cloth.

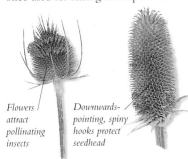

Flowers attract pollinating insects

Downwards-pointing, spiny hooks protect seedhead

BIRD USE Only goldfinches and crossbills have bills that are long and slender enough to extract seeds from the narrow tubes of petals.

WILD STRAWBERRY

Fragaria vesca

The wild strawberry is a perennial herb that spreads by runners, which take root and form fresh plants. It grows in woods and grassland where soil is rich in organic matter. The white flowers open between April and July and ripen into fleshy, red fruits.
HEIGHT AND SPREAD 10–20 cm.
CULTIVATION Grow in fertile, moist but well-drained soil in full sun or light-dappled shade. Protect flowers from frost with a straw mulch.
RELATED *F.* x *ananassa* 'Aromel', a "perpetual" cultivar, bears a second crop in autumn. Alpine cultivars fruit from mid-summer to autumn.

Soft, sweet fruits attract wide range of birds

Seeds cover fruit's surface

BIRD USE Seeds and flesh of fruits are eaten by woodpigeons, thrushes, crows, sparrows, blackcaps, linnets, chaffinches, and greenfinches.

FIELD FORGET-ME-NOT

Myosotis arvensis

The field forget-me-not is a small annual or biennial that grows rapidly on cultivated ground, coastal dunes, or bare waste land. It is commonly regarded as a weed. Small, bright blue flowers are borne from April to September, followed by seed clusters.
HEIGHT 15 cm. **SPREAD** 10 cm.
CULTIVATION Grow in moderately fertile or poor soil that is well drained. Cultivated forms are sown as seed in autumn, or bought as bedding plants.
RELATED Water forget-me-not (*M. scorpoides*) is suitable for bog gardens and pond margins. *M. sylvatica* is a popular cultivated species.

Birds feed on resident slugs and snails.

Tiny seeds are popular with finches

BIRD USE The autumn nutlets, or seeds, are eaten by chaffinches, reed buntings, serins, linnets, goldfinches, bullfinches, and greenfinches.

HERBACEOUS PLANTS

EVENING PRIMROSE

Oenothera biennis

Evening primrose is a biennial herb that can often thrive on sand dunes, railway embankments, and similar dry sites. It is grown in gardens for its succession of short-lived, yellow flowers, which open in the evening. The fruit capsule contains numerous seeds that self-sow easily.
HEIGHT 1 m. **SPREAD** 40 cm.
CULTIVATION Grow in poor to quite fertile, well-drained soil in full sun. Increase plants by division in spring.
RELATED *O. acaulis*, which matures from white to pink, and Ozark sundrops (*O. macrocarpa*) grow to 15 cm high and suit small gardens.

Bright yellow flowers attract insects

Birds are attracted to tiny seeds inside capsules

BIRD USE Insects on the flowers attract warblers. Seeds are eaten by crossbills, chaffinches, bramblings, greenfinches, goldfinches, serins, and siskins.

COMMON BISTORT

Persicaria bistorta

Bistort and its wild relatives are weeds, commonly seen growing in meadows and on verges. This vigorous, clump-forming perennial may be invasive in gardens. Spikes of pink flowers open from June to August, followed by brownish-red fruits in autumn.
HEIGHT to 50 cm. **SPREAD** 40 cm.
CULTIVATION Grow in any moist soil in full sun or part shade. The flower spikes may be cut after seeding.
RELATED Wild relatives include knotgrass (*P. aviculare*) and viviparous bistort (*P. vivipara*), a northern region species. *P. affinis* is a cultivated bistort that provides winter colour.

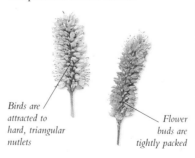

Birds are attracted to hard, triangular nutlets

Flower buds are tightly packed

BIRD USE Seeds are eaten by collared doves, pheasants, black-headed gulls, dunnocks, finches, crows, and sparrows. Bulbils of *P. vivipara* are eaten by birds.

GROUNDSEL

Senecio vulgaris

An annual weed that sometimes survives the winter, groundsel invades waste land and cultivated ground alike, and flourishes in flowerbeds. Its clusters of small, yellow flowers are quickly followed by globes of hairy seeds that are dispersed on the wind. The early flowering period makes groundsel a useful food for birds in late winter and early spring.
HEIGHT 30 cm. **SPREAD** 10 cm.
CULTIVATION Grow in any soil. Self-seeds easily. Cultivated varieties need moderately fertile soil in full sun.
RELATED *S. cineraria* and cultivars have silvery-green, felted leaves.

Fluffy seedheads are dispersed by wind

BIRD USE Seeds are eaten throughout the year by a wide range of garden birds, including bullfinches, linnets, greenfinches, and goldfinches.

DANDELION
Taraxacum officinale

A perennial herb and fast-spreading weed, the dandelion favours open spaces and thrives in herbaceous beds. Its solitary, yellow flowers appear from February to October, bringing colour to lawns. However, the flat leaf-rosettes displace grass and the deep taproots are difficult to eradicate. If the flowers are allowed to go to seed, an invasion of dandelions often results later in the year. The seedhead, or clock, contains numerous white, hairy seeds that are dispersed on the wind.
HEIGHT 30 cm. **SPREAD** 15 cm.
CULTIVATION Self-seeds freely.
RELATED No cultivated varieties.

Bright yellow flowers attract insects

Leaves are eaten by woodpigeons

BIRD USE The early seed crop is valuable to bullfinches, greenfinches, goldfinches, and serins. Woodpigeons eat the flowers and leaves.

RED CLOVER
Trifolium pratense

Clover is a low-growing, perennial herb that grows wild in meadows or scrub and is also used as a forage crop. Although it is considered a weed in lawns, clover makes a colourful addition to wildflower gardens and attracts bumblebees. Round heads of pink-purple flowers appear in late spring and summer, and the seeds ripen in tiny pods. Clover is an effective improver of soil fertility.
HEIGHT 20 cm. **SPREAD** 20 cm.
CULTIVATION Grow in well-drained soil in full sun. Self-seeds easily.
RELATED *T. incarnatum* has deep red to creamy-yellow flowers.

Birds search through flowers for pollinating insects

Pigeons and bullfinches eat leaves

BIRD USE Ripe seeds are eaten by several garden birds, such as finches. Bullfinches and woodpigeons eat the leaves as well as the seeds. .

COMMON NETTLE
Urtica dioica

The common nettle is a perennial herb that grows in open country and woods, and on waste land, often near buildings. Vigorous growth and stinging leaves make it an unpopular weed, but its value to caterpillars and other insects makes the plant essential in a wildlife garden. Inconspicuous, greenish flowers, hanging like slender catkins, appear from June to August.
HEIGHT 1.5 m. **SPREAD** 15 cm.
CULTIVATION Grow in a confined area. Cut mature stems to promote fresh growth for caterpillars.
RELATED Annual nettle (*U. urens*) is a smaller, less-invasive species.

Hairy leaves attract caterpillars

Seeds are eaten by birds

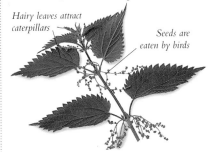

BIRD USE Seeds are eaten by reed buntings, bullfinches, serins, and siskins. Resident insects, especially caterpillars, attract many garden birds.

ADDITIONAL PLANTS

Below are additional planting suggestions of hardy varieties that tolerate a wide range of conditions. Like the plants on the previous pages, they are not exclusive to this region, and many of them can be cultivated successfully elsewhere in Europe.

TREES

COMMON HORNBEAM

Carpinus betulus

Hornbeam is a small, deciduous tree that is suitable for use as hedging. It is often mistaken for beech in winter, but can be distinguished by its yellow-green male catkins and saw-toothed leaves at other times of the year. The female catkins develop into small, winged nutlets. They ripen in autumn and remain on the tree through the winter. Young trees of less than 3 m high retain their dead leaves in winter. **HEIGHT** 25 m. **SPREAD** 20 m. **CULTIVATION** Plant in sun or part shade between October and March. Keep the young plant moist until it is well established. Clip straggly branches in July to keep the tree's shape. **RELATED** *C. b.* 'Columnaris' and *C. b.* 'Fastigiata' suit small gardens. **BIRD USE** The nutlets are eaten by ring-necked parakeets, mallards, tits, great spotted woodpeckers, rooks, nuthatches, jays, and finches.

COMMON PEAR

Pyrus communis

This small, sometimes thorny, deciduous tree is found in woods and hedges across much of Europe. Its deep roots enable the tree to make the best of poor soils. Pear is widely grown for its white, often pink-tinged blossoms borne in spring, and for its edible fruits, which are produced in late summer and autumn. Cultivated varieties can be raised as trees or bushes, or trained against walls. **HEIGHT** 15 m. **SPREAD** 10 m.

CULTIVATION Grow in fertile, well-drained soil in a warm site. Shelter from frost and salty coastal winds. **RELATED** *P. c.* 'Conference', a late-flowering variety, prefers cold climates. **BIRD USE** Fruits and seeds are eaten by moorhens, jays, tits, nuthatches, fieldfares, lesser-spotted woodpeckers, magpies, woodpigeons, waxwings, starlings, finches, and thrushes.

YEW

Taxus baccata

Yew is an evergreen tree or shrub that is grown for its dense foliage of dark green, flattened leaves and reddish-brown bark. It is suitable for growing as a boundary hedge and tolerates sun or shade, drought, exposure, and polluted air. The male and female flowers are borne on separate trees. Yellow, male cones are produced in spring, while the female flower develops into a bright red, cup-shaped fruit, which ripens from late August. Note: all parts are poisonous if eaten. **HEIGHT** 15 m. **SPREAD** 10 m. **CULTIVATION** Grow in any well-drained soil, in sun or shade. **RELATED** *T. b.* 'Dovastonii Aurea' bears golden foliage and grows to between 3 m and 5 m high. **BIRD USE** Fruits are eaten by robins, moorhens, woodpigeons, waxwings, redstarts, thrushes, jays, great spotted woodpeckers, starlings, blackcaps, tits, nuthatches, and finches.

SHRUBS

JAPANESE QUINCE

Chaenomeles japonica

This deciduous, thorny shrub can be used as hedging or ground cover. It is grown for its clusters of showy, red flowers borne in spring. Edible, yellow fruits that resemble apples are produced in autumn. **HEIGHT** 1 m. **SPREAD** 2 m.

CULTIVATION Grow in well-drained soil in sun. Sow seed or layer in autumn, or take cuttings in summer. **RELATED** *C. speciosa* is a larger species with tangled, spiny branches. **BIRD USE** Blackbirds and starlings eat the fruits. Bullfinches eat the flowers.

GOOSEBERRY

Ribes uva-crispa

This branching, spiny shrub grows in woods, thickets, and hedges. Small, green, purple-tinged flowers open in March and April, followed by sour, green fruits from May to August. **HEIGHT** 1.5 m. **SPREAD** 75 cm. **CULTIVATION** Grow in sun or part shade, avoiding exposed sites. Keep the roots moist and prune the bush to improve fruiting and prevent mildew. It is best grown as a bush or trained on wire or against a fence. **RELATED** A vigorous bush, *R. u-c.* 'Invicta' is immune to mildew. **BIRD USE** Nectar is sipped by blue tits. Fruits are eaten by blackbirds.

SNOWBERRY

Symphoricarpos albus var. *laevigatus*

Snowberry is a small, deciduous shrub that has become widely naturalized, especially in damp places. It is a hardy plant that is tolerant of poor soils. Small, pink flowers are produced in summer, but it is primarily grown for its clusters of large, white berries, which stay on the branches in winter. Note: the fruits are poisonous if eaten and may irritate the skin on contact. **HEIGHT** 2 m. **SPREAD** 2 m. **CULTIVATION** Grow in rich, moist soil in sun or part shade. **RELATED** Coralberry or Indian currant (*S. orbiculatus*) yields a large crop of berries after a hot summer. **BIRD USE** Berries are eaten by robins, waxwings, fieldfares, garden warblers, tits, blackbirds, blackcaps, and finches.

Herbaceous Plants

Amaranth

Amaranthus caudatus

Commonly known as love-lies-bleeding, amaranth is tolerant of poor soil. It is grown for its long tassels (45 cm) of crimson flowers, which open from July to October. Coloured seedheads appear after the flowering.
HEIGHT 1.2 m. **SPREAD** 45 cm.
CULTIVATION Sow seeds under glass in March, or sow direct in full sun in a sheltered site in April.
RELATED Joseph's coat (*A. tricolor*) is grown for its multicoloured foliage.
BIRD USE Seeds are eaten by collared doves, dunnocks, sparrows, magpies, reed buntings, and finches.

Michaelmas Daisy

Aster novi-belgii

Introduced from North America as a garden plant, the michaelmas daisy has become naturalized in much of Europe. It is a tall, branching perennial that often grows near water or in damp places. Clusters of violet flowers with yellow discs are produced in September and October.
HEIGHT 1 m. **SPREAD** 50 cm.
CULTIVATION Grow in moist soil in sun. Stake taller plants. Propagate by cuttings or divide established plants in spring or summer.
RELATED *A. tradescantii* bears white autumn flowers. *A. alpinus* is suitable for growing in a rock garden.
BIRD USE Seeds are eaten by siskins, linnets, crossbills, and other finches.

Fat Hen

Chenopodium album

A member of the goosefoot family, this tall, annual weed colonizes bare ground, and can be found on waste ground, farmland, and in gardens. Fat hen is also cultivated to provide food for gamebirds. Flowers are produced from June to October, followed by small seeds, which are available through the winter, either on the plant or dispersed on the ground.

HEIGHT 1 m. **SPREAD** 30 cm.
CULTIVATION Sow seeds of the cultivated variety in spring.
RELATED Good King Henry (*C. bonus-henricus*) bears flower spikes.
BIRD USE Seeds are eaten by pheasants, woodpigeons, collared doves, dunnocks, and finches.

St John's Wort

Hypericum perforatum

This evergreen, perennial herb or shrub is common in woods and shady places. It spreads by underground stems and can become a garden weed. A mass of star-shaped, yellow flowers is borne from June to September. Note: all parts are poisonous if eaten.
HEIGHT 90 cm. **SPREAD** Indefinite.
CULTIVATION Grow in moist soil in sun or part shade. Propagate by cuttings in spring or autumn.
RELATED *H. reptans* suits sunny walls or rock gardens. Rose of Sharon (*H. calycinum*) is good ground cover.
BIRD USE Seeds are eaten by blackcaps, bullfinches, and redpolls.

Perennial Flax

Linum perenne

Perennial flax is a clump-forming plant that grows wild in grasslands and mountains. Sky-blue flowers are produced in abundance from June to August, followed by oily, brown seeds.
HEIGHT 30 cm. **SPREAD** 15 cm.
CULTIVATION Sow seed in September or March in full sun. Flax grows easily.
RELATED Golden flax (*L. flavum*) is a bushy perennial with yellow flowers.
BIRD USE Seeds are eaten by sparrows, woodpigeons, siskins, linnets, and other finches.

Corn Poppy

Papaver rhoeas

This tall, annual herb can be recognized by its large, scarlet flowers. Corn poppies grow on waste ground and in fields. They are also common in gardens. The flowers open from May to July, falling to leave behind a "pepperpot" fruit packed full of small seeds. The seeds often lie dormant in the soil for many years. When the ground is disturbed, they germinate and rise to the surface.
HEIGHT 90 cm. **SPREAD** 10 cm.
CULTIVATION Sow seeds in well-drained soil in sun or part shade. Poppies self-seed readily.
RELATED Oriental poppy (*P. orientale*) and opium poppy (*P. somniferum*) are suitable for gardens.
BIRD USE Seeds are eaten by dunnocks, jackdaws, sparrows, siskins, linnets, and other finches.

Primrose

Primula vulgaris

This herbaceous perennial grows in meadows and open woods, and on shady banks. The colourful flowers are borne on individual stems from March to May. Seeds are shed from the withered flowerheads in late summer.
HEIGHT 20 cm. **SPREAD** 20 cm.
CULTIVATION Plant in moisture-retentive soil in sun or part shade between September and March. Trim the foliage and remove the seedheads after the seeds have been dispersed.
RELATED Many species and cultivated varieties of *Primula* are suitable for growing in borders or in patio tubs or containers.
BIRD USE Seeds are eaten by chaffinches. Sparrows are known to attack the colourful petals.

Sweet Violet

Viola odorata

This clump-forming, semi-evergreen perennial can be found growing in woods and hedgerows. It is ideal for planting in raised beds, wildflower gardens, or pots. Scented, violet or white flowers open in spring, and often again in autumn.
HEIGHT 7 cm. **SPREAD** 15 cm.
CULTIVATION Grow in moist but well-drained soil in sun or part shade.
RELATED Heartsease or wild pansy (*V. tricolor*) and garden pansies (*V. x wittrockiana*) offer a range of colours.
BIRD USE Seeds are eaten by coal tits, woodpigeons, and bullfinches.

NORTHERN REGION

LONG, COLD WINTERS with short periods of daylight and a limited growing season present special problems for gardeners in the northern region. In some parts of Scandinavia, gardens are often enclosed clearings in woodland rather than landscaped plots. The amount of sunlight reaching the ground in these areas is limited even at the height of summer. Moreover, competition for nutrients and water between the surrounding trees weakens the soil.

Use trees and shrubs in a planting scheme for this region, since these will give structure to a garden and will act as windbreaks, even when leafless in winter. To minimize plant loss, try to use only species that are fully hardy.

Many birds migrate away from this region in winter to warmer climates. Even so, any scraps and seeds scattered in your garden will be valued by those birds that stay behind and eagerly sought by migrants when they return at the end of winter.

Cracking Open Cherries
Shattered fruit stones found beneath a bird cherry tree are a sure sign that hawfinches have been cracking open the fruits with their large bills to extract kernels.

FRUIT BORDER
Scrambling fruits like blackberry can be invasive and untidy-looking, so train them to grow on a trellis.

CENTRAL BED
Birds can use the foliage for cover and perching when visiting the birdbath and birdtable.

Foraging for Food
Low-growing bilberries and crowberries have attracted this pheasant, which is foraging in the garden borders.

WHAT TO PLANT

Fill borders with flowering fruits, from low-growing crowberries to scrambling blackberries. Together with cobnut trees, these provide crops that can be enjoyed by birds and humans alike. Plant a selection of annuals to provide colour in the garden, and grow roses and rhododendrons as bedding or pot plants so that they can be placed under cover during winter.

WOODLAND AREA
Grow native grasses and flowers beneath trees, since they adapt well to poor soil and light.

Cone Feast
Alder cones are an important source of food for siskins, which use their slender bills to extract the seeds.

GARDEN PATH
Bark chippings provide interest and texture on woodland paths or act as a mulch on flowerbeds.

PLANTING LIST

Clockwise from bottom left

LEFT FRUIT BORDER
Dwarf willow, blackberry, blackcurrant, meadowsweet, angelica

WOODLAND AREA
Bird cherry, alder, cobnut, rowan, silver birch

RIGHT FRUIT BORDER
Blackcurrant, bilberry, blackberry, crowberry

PATIO
Roses, selection of annuals

CENTRAL BED
Yarrow, angelica, meadowsweet

TREES

COMMON ALDER

Alnus glutinosa

Alder is a medium-sized, deciduous tree that often lines the banks of streams and lakes, or forms woods in marshy ground. Alder suits coppicing (*see p. 29*) but is not recommended for small gardens. The yellow (male) and red (female) catkins ripen together on the same branches, and appear in early spring before the leaves. The woody cones ripen to brown in autumn.

HEIGHT 25 m. **SPREAD** 10 m.

CULTIVATION Grow in moderately fertile, moist, well-drained soil in sun.

RELATED Italian alder (*A. cordata*) and grey alder (*A. incana*) are fast-growing and tolerate poor, dry soils.

Fruits open in dry winter weather

Birds extract seeds from cones

BIRD USE Seeds are eaten by reed buntings, long-tailed tits, marsh tits, coal tits, waxwings, and finches. Both seeds and buds are eaten by siskins.

SILVER BIRCH

Betula pendula

The small, deciduous birch tree forms colonies in open ground and tolerates exposed sites. It is grown for its golden leaves in autumn and its peeling, white bark. The slender, drooping twigs bear yellow, hanging (male) and green, upright (female) catkins, which open in April and May. When mature, the trunks are ideal for nesting holes.

HEIGHT 20 m. **SPREAD** 10 m.

CULTIVATION Grow in dry soil in sun. Birch will tolerate acid and poor soil. Site clear of other trees and walls, since its roots grow near the surface.

RELATED Monarch birch (*B. maximowicziana*) is quick-growing.

Serins eat catkins

Birch leaves attract aphids

BIRD USE Winged seeds are eaten by waxwings, dunnocks, tits, jays, crows, magpies, sparrows, reed buntings, finches, chiffchaffs, and other warblers.

BIRD CHERRY

Prunus padus

Bird cherry is a small, deciduous tree or bush that grows in woods and on coastal sites. The flowers develop into bitter-tasting, black cherries that ripen in July and August. The tree often produces a tangle of crowded shoots, known as witches' broom, which causes the leaves to discolour.

HEIGHT 6 m. **SPREAD** 6 m.

CULTIVATION Grow in any moist but well-drained soil in full sun. Shallow roots prevent underplanting.

RELATED Wild cherry (*P. avium*), the ancestor of cultivated cherries, is most common in the southern region. Some varieties do not produce fruits.

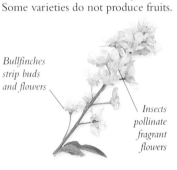

Bullfinches strip buds and flowers

Insects pollinate fragrant flowers

BIRD USE The flesh of cherries is eaten by most birds, but hawfinches also eat the stones. Tits and warblers are attracted by pollinating insects.

SHRUBS AND CLIMBERS

ROWAN

Sorbus aucuparia

Also known as mountain ash, rowan is a slender, deciduous tree that is found on open moorland, and in woods and scrub. It is tolerant of atmospheric pollution. Red or orange berries are borne in heavy clusters after the flowers. Migrations of fieldfares and waxwings in autumn may be delayed if a good crop of berries is produced.
HEIGHT 15 m. **SPREAD** 8 m.
CULTIVATION Grow in moderately fertile, well-drained soil in full sun or light-dappled shade.
RELATED Wild service tree (*S. torminalis*) and whitebeam (*S. aria*) are suitable for growing in gardens.

Insect-eating birds are attracted to resident aphids

Paired leaves turn red in autumn

BIRD USE Berries are eaten by nuthatches, thrushes, tits, waxwings, starlings, crows, sparrows, blackcaps, crossbills, and other finches.

COBNUT

Corylus avellana

A member of the hazel family, this deciduous shrub sometimes grows into a tree. It is found in hedgerows, scrub, coppices, and as undergrowth in woods. The long, yellow catkins (male), known as lambs' tails, appear in January with the less-conspicuous female flowers, which resemble buds.
HEIGHT 6 m. **SPREAD** 6 m.
CULTIVATION Cobnut suits chalky soil. Grow in well-drained, fertile soil in sun or part shade. Nuts are borne after 7 years. Remove suckers in May.
RELATED The twisted shoots of Corkscrew hazel (*C. a.* 'Contorta', *shown above*) are used for decoration.

Birds feed on catkins

Cobnuts are eaten by many birds

BIRD USE Nuts are eaten by pheasants, great spotted woodpeckers, nuthatches, tits, jackdaws, jays, hawfinches, and crossbills.

CROWBERRY

Empetrum nigrum

This small, evergreen shrub can be mistaken for a member of the heather family. Crowberry grows on moors and heaths, and in open woodland, where it provides good ground cover for birds. It has small, dense leaves and many stems, which take root where they touch the ground. The pink flowers open from April to June, followed by glossy, black fruits that remain on the plant during winter.
HEIGHT 45 cm. **SPREAD** 30 cm.
CULTIVATION Grow in acid soil, preferably on open ground.
RELATED *E. n.* 'Lucia' produces creamy-white shoots.

Glossy berries attract birds

Dense-leaved stems provide ground cover

BIRD USE Berries are eaten by gulls, waxwings, marsh tits, woodpigeons, redstarts, fieldfares, flycatchers, crows, chaffinches, bramblings, and crossbills.

SHRUBS AND CLIMBERS

BLACKCURRANT

Ribes nigrum

Blackcurrant is a deciduous shrub that grows in woods and hedgerows. Many garden varieties are available. The dull-green flowers open in April and May, followed by small, round currants that are protected by prickly branches.
HEIGHT 2 m. **SPREAD** 2 m.
CULTIVATION Grow in moderately fertile soil in full sun. Cut out old stems in winter to retain plant's shape.
RELATED *R. n.* 'Ben Lomond' (*shown above*), redcurrant (*R. rubrum*), and gooseberry (*R. uva-crispa*) are grown for their fruits. Flowering currant (*R. sanguineum*) bears nectar-rich flowers but often fails to fruit.

BLACKBERRY

Rubus fruticosus

Blackberry, or bramble, is a perennial, deciduous climber that grows wild in woods and hedgerows. When left untrimmed, it forms an impenetrable thicket that is ideal for nesting. White flowers are borne in summer, followed by plump, black fruits in early autumn.
HEIGHT 3 m. **SPREAD** 3 m.
CULTIVATION Grow in well-drained, moderately fertile soil, preferably in full sun. Train against a wall or wires if grown for fruits. Cut stems to the ground after fruiting.
RELATED Dewberry (*R. caesius*), cloudberry (*R. chamaemorus*), and raspberry (*R. idaeus*) bear edible fruits.

BILBERRY

Vaccinium myrtillus

Also known as a whortleberry or whinberry, this small, deciduous shrub bears leathery, bright green leaves. It commonly grows on acid moorland and heaths, and in woods. It is suitable for growing in woodland gardens. Pink, bell-shaped flowers open from April to June and the sweet-tasting berries ripen from July to September.
HEIGHT 60 cm. **SPREAD** 30 cm.
CULTIVATION Grow in acid, peat-rich, or sandy, moist but well-drained soil in full sun or part shade.
RELATED Cowberry (*V. vitis-idaea*) is an evergreen shrub. Cranberry (*V. macrocarpon*) needs cool, moist soil.

Birds are attracted to fruits

Branch structure is good for nesting

Dense brambles provide secure nesting site

Plump berries attract birds

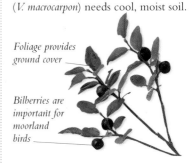

Foliage provides ground cover

Bilberries are important for moorland birds

BIRD USE Currants are eaten by woodpigeons, waxwings, flycatchers, tits, jays, sparrows, magpies, warblers, finches, blackbirds, and thrushes.

BIRD USE Berries are eaten by crows, woodpigeons, flycatchers, nuthatches, finches, starlings, thrushes, blackcaps, waxwings, pheasants, and moorhens.

BIRD USE Berries are eaten by black-headed gulls, woodpigeons, waxwings, thrushes, crows, warblers, chaffinches, bramblings, siskins, and crossbills.

HERBACEOUS PLANTS

YARROW

Achillea millefolium

Yarrow, also commonly known as milfoil, has finely divided leaves. This perennial, scented herb can be found in hedgerows and grassland, and by roadsides. It is ideal for growing in a wildflower or rock garden, but may be invasive. Clusters of white flowers bloom from June to November.
HEIGHT 60 cm. **SPREAD** 60 cm.
CULTIVATION Grow in moist but well-drained soil in full sun, either in an open site or in a container. Stake the stems, especially when grown in exposed positions.
RELATED *A. m.* 'Fire King' is vigorous and has red flowerheads.

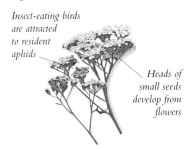

Insect-eating birds are attracted to resident aphids

Heads of small seeds develop from flowers

BIRD USE Seeds are eaten by house sparrows, tits, chaffinches, bullfinches, and greenfinches. Birds feed on pollinating insects on the flowers.

ANGELICA

Angelica sylvestris

Angelica is a tall, perennial herb that is common in damp places. It is best grown in a large border or by a pond or stream. The white or pink flowers open from July to September in the third year, followed by winged fruits. The flowers are insect-pollinated and attract large numbers of insects.
HEIGHT 2 m. **SPREAD** 1 m.
CULTIVATION Grow in deep, moist, fertile loam soil, preferably in full sun. Allow seeds to form after flowering. Angelica is best grown as a biennial.
RELATED Archangel (*A. archangelica*) is a native of northern Europe that has become naturalized in many areas.

Foliage hosts slugs, snails, and aphids

Purple stems are deeply ribbed

BIRD USE Seeds are eaten by blue tits and greenfinches. Many birds are attracted to pests on the plants and pollinating insects on the flowers.

MEADOWSWEET

Filipendula ulmaria

Meadowsweet, also known as queen of the meadows, is a perennial herb that grows in wet places such as water meadows and marshes, and on river banks. It is also suitable for naturalizing in a woodland garden. The dense clusters of fragrant, creamy-white flowers open from June to September and ripen into single-seeded fruits that twist together in tight bunches.
HEIGHT 1.2 m. **SPREAD** 1 m.
CULTIVATION Grow in moist soil in full sun or part shade.
RELATED *F. u.* 'Aurea' has golden foliage. Dropwort (*F. vulgaris*) is shorter (60 cm) with larger flowers.

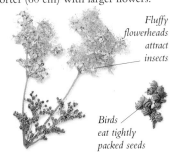

Fluffy flowerheads attract insects

Birds eat tightly packed seeds

BIRD USE Seeds are eaten by linnets, reed buntings, siskins, chaffinches, hawfinches, and bullfinches. Extensive drifts of the plant provide good cover.

ADDITIONAL PLANTS

Below are additional planting suggestions of hardy varieties that tolerate a wide range of conditions. Like the plants on the previous pages, they are not exclusive to this region, and many of them can be cultivated successfully elsewhere in Europe.

TREES

COMMON ASH

Fraxinus excelsior

Ash is a tall, deciduous tree that grows well on alkaline soils. It is resistant to wind and air pollution and is suitable for growing in woodland or coastal gardens. Ash is one of the last trees to come into leaf and one of the first to shed its foliage. Clusters of flowers appear before the leaves and give a purple tinge to the tree. The winged fruits, or keys, ripen in late summer and remain on the tree until spring.
HEIGHT 30 m. **SPREAD** 20 m.
CULTIVATION Grow in well-drained, fertile soil in full sun.
RELATED White ash (*F. americana*) is fast-growing. The branches of weeping ash (*F. e.* 'Pendula') often reach down to the ground.
BIRD USE Seeds are eaten by finches, waxwings, woodpigeons, great spotted woodpeckers, and tits.

COMMON LIME

Tilia × europaea

The lime is a tall, deciduous tree, which is widely planted in avenues, parks, and gardens. The flowers open in June and July, followed by hard, downy seeds, which ripen in October. Lime-tree leaves are attacked by aphids, which coat the foliage and ground below with honeydew.
HEIGHT 35 m. **SPREAD** 15 m.
CULTIVATION Grow in moist but well-drained, preferably alkaline or neutral soil in sun or part shade. Lime trees are suitable for lopping and for coppicing (*see p. 29*).

RELATED Both pendent silver lime (*T.* 'Petiolaris') and silver lime (*T. tomentosa*) produce leaves with silver undersides. The flower nectar of both species is poisonous to bees.
BIRD USE Insect-eating species are attracted to the bees and aphids. Seeds are eaten by waxwings and finches.

SMOOTH-LEAVED ELM

Ulmus minor

This tall, deciduous tree is commonly found in hedgerows, woodlands, and thickets. Unfortunately, it is vulnerable to Dutch elm disease, which is fatal. Elms are considered to be a nuisance in gardens because of their habit of growing readily from suckers at the roots. Clusters of small, bell-shaped red flowers appear before the leaves in February or March. These are followed by green, winged seeds, which ripen and fall during summer.
HEIGHT 30 m. **SPREAD** 20 m.
CULTIVATION Grow in well-drained soil in sun or part shade. Elms can be propagated from suckers.
RELATED English elm (*U. procera*) is native to Britain. Wych elm (*U. glabra*) is propagated by seed not suckers.
BIRD USE Seeds are eaten by moorhens, woodpigeons, waxwings, sparrow, siskins, and other finches.

SHRUBS

SCOTS HEATHER

Calluna vulgaris

Heathers are hardy, evergreen, woody shrubs that grow on moorland and heaths. They spread to form dense mats of ground cover and are very attractive to bees. Lilac bell-shaped flowers are borne in mid-summer.
HEIGHT 30 cm. **SPREAD** 45 cm.
CULTIVATION Grow in well-drained, acid soil in full sun. Take semi-ripe cuttings in mid-summer, or layer in spring. Trim lightly to keep compact.

RELATED Winter heath (*Erica carnea*) flowers through winter and is lime-tolerant. Bell heather (*E. cinerea*) needs warm, dry, acid soil.
BIRD USE Seeds are eaten by siskins, crossbills, and other finches.

HERBACEOUS PLANTS

CORNFLOWER

Centaurea cyanus

Cornflowers were once regarded as problem weeds in cornfields, but they have been almost eradicated by grain-cleaning methods. They are ideal for naturalizing in grass or for attracting bees and butterflies to a wildflower garden. Bright blue flowers are produced between June and August.
HEIGHT 1 m. **SPREAD** 30 cm.
CULTIVATION Sow seed in well-drained soil either in spring or in late summer to flower early in the following year. Grow cornflowers in pots for winter-flowering plants.
RELATED Perennial cornflower (*C. montana*) spreads vigorously and may need staking when in flower.
BIRD USE Seeds are eaten by blue tits, carrion crows, greenfinches, siskins, goldfinches, linnets, and crossbills.

GREATER KNAPWEED

Centaurea scabiosa

Greater knapweed is a thistle-like perennial found growing in sparse woods, pastures, and verges. It is a colourful weed in gardens, where several of its relatives are grown as herbaceous plants. Solitary, reddish-purple flowers borne in summer are attractive to bees and butterflies.
HEIGHT 90 cm. **SPREAD** 30 cm.
CULTIVATION Grow on open ground, preferably in lime, in full sun. Propagate by dividing the plant during spring or autumn, or by sowing seed in spring.

RELATED Common knapweed (*C. nigra*) flowers from June onwards.
BIRD USE Seeds are eaten by blue tits, carrion crows, goldfinches, siskins, linnets, greenfinches, and crossbills.

COMMON MOUSE-EAR

Cerastium fontanum

This carpet-forming, perennial herb is a common weed found in grassy and moist places. It is suitable for growing in border fronts and rock gardens, and on walls. White, star-shaped flowers open between April and November, followed by fruit capsules. These produce large numbers of small seeds, which remain viable for many years.
HEIGHT 45 cm. **SPREAD** Indefinite.
CULTIVATION Grow in any well-drained soil in full sun. Common mouse-ear spreads easily and can be propagated by seed or cuttings.
RELATED Snow-in-summer (*C. tomentosum*) tolerates poor soil and grows well on dry, sunny banks, but tends to become rampant.
BIRD USE Seeds are eaten by woodpigeons, reed buntings, siskins, linnets, and other finches.

WILLOW HERB

Epilobium angustifolium

This tall, perennial herb grows in open woods, and on heaths and waste land. It is often seen on burnt ground, hence its other common name of fireweed. Bright, pink-purple flowers are produced in summer, making it one of the most attractive garden weeds. A mass of bedraggled seedheads releases thousands of feathery seeds during autumn.
HEIGHT 1.2 m. **SPREAD** 50 cm.
CULTIVATION Sow cultivated varieties in autumn in fertile, well-drained soil on sunny banks and in rock gardens. Willow herb is prone to slugs and snails, which are welcome food for visiting birds.
RELATED *E. glabellum* of gardens makes good ground cover and prefers cool, damp shade. White rosebay (*E. a.* f. *album*) produces white flowers in late summer and self-seeds freely.

BIRD USE Seeds are eaten by house sparrows, reed buntings, siskins, linnets, crossbills, and other finches.

REED

Phragmites australis

This tall, smooth-stemmed perennial lives in shallow water and waterlogged soil. It forms dense clumps of narrow, pointed leaves and tends to be invasive. The feathery, purple-brown flowers borne in late summer and autumn are suitable for use in dried flower arrangements and indoor decoration.
HEIGHT 3 m. **SPREAD** Indefinite.
CULTIVATION Reeds are best grown in containers under water so as to restrict their growth. They can be propagated by division in early spring.
RELATED *P. a.* 'Variegatus' has gold-striped leaves that fade to white.
BIRD USE Flowers are used as nest material by many water birds and the leaves provide good cover.

GREATER PLANTAIN

Plantago major

Plantain is a perennial herb that grows in mown or grazed grassland. It is a common sight on lawns and gravel paths in gardens. A spike of small, greenish-yellow flowers emerges in spring from a flat rosette of leaves, followed by a capsule of small seeds.
HEIGHT 30 cm. **SPREAD** 60 cm.
CULTIVATION Grow in sharply drained soil that is preferably neutral to acid, in full sun. Greater plantain spreads easily and tends to be invasive.
RELATED *P. nivalis* is a compact species that suits rock gardens.
BIRD USE Seeds are eaten by woodpigeons, starlings, dunnocks, sparrows, siskins, and other finches.

CREEPING BUTTERCUP

Ranunculus repens

Creeping buttercups grow in damp meadows and woods, and spread rapidly across lawns and untended beds. The bright yellow flowers borne from May to August attract insects.
HEIGHT 5 cm. **SPREAD** 20 cm.

CULTIVATION Grow in moist, fertile soil in full or part shade. Sow seed in autumn or divide in spring. Creeping buttercups are prone to slugs, snails, and aphids, all of which attract birds.
RELATED Lesser celandine (*R. ficaria*) is suitable for wild gardens. Greater spearwort (*R. lingua*) is a marginal plant that suits water gardens.
BIRD USE Seeds are eaten by moorhens, woodpigeons, dunnocks, jackdaws, redpolls, and other finches. Leaves are eaten by woodpigeons.

CURLED DOCK

Rumex crispus

This vigorous perennial is a renowned, invasive weed on arable farmland and it also spreads readily in gardens. Dense heads of greenish, star-shaped flowers appear between June and October, followed by small, triangular, red-brown fruits.
HEIGHT 1 m. **SPREAD** 15 cm.
CULTIVATION Grow in moderately fertile, well-drained soil in sun. Curled dock self-seeds easily, but seeds may be sown in spring.
RELATED Sorrel (*R. acetosa*), sheep's sorrel (*R. acetosella*), and water dock (*R. aquatica*) are all grown as herbs.
BIRD USE Seeds are eaten by reed buntings, jackdaws, and finches.

COMMON CHICKWEED

Stellaria media

Chickweed has traditionally been grown as food for game birds and domestic fowl in many countries. It is found on waste land and in grass verges and gardens. Chickweed usually straggles on the ground. Small, white, star-shaped flowers and drooping seed capsules are borne all year round.
HEIGHT 90 cm. **SPREAD** 60 cm.
CULTIVATION Grow in moist soil in sun or shade. Seed may be sown at any time of the year.
RELATED Greater chickweed (*S. neglecta*) is common in central and southern Europe.
BIRD USE Seeds are eaten by linnets, woodpigeons, bramblings, siskins, greenfinches, redpolls, and waxwings.

SOUTHERN REGION

THE MEDITERRANEAN climate of the southern region is characterized by mild, wet winters and dry, hot summers. A dense cover of evergreen, drought-resistant small trees and shrubs often dominates the landscape.

In the garden, periods of plant growth are usually limited to spring and autumn because the summer is too dry. Grass lawns are rarely cultivated because they would require very frequent watering throughout the summer months. Paving and gravel are often used to surface the main area, edged with ground cover for easy maintenance. Scented plants, such as lavender and marjoram, are typical of the southern region and suit displays in central beds. A large population of resident insects in the garden attracts birds during summer, while berries draw in winter migrants from the northern region, such as warblers and thrushes.

Tasty Catch
A winter migrant to the southern region, this garden warbler is feeding on insects on a fig tree.

TERRACE
Paved areas are more practical to maintain than grass lawns in dry climates.

PERGOLA
A vine-clad pergola offers cool shade at the back of a house.

Sunflower Seeds
A seed-eating bird, this collared dove is enjoying the tightly packed seeds of a cut sunflower head.

WHAT TO PLANT
Mulberry, olive, and fig trees, interspersed with sunflowers, barberry, and juniper, ensure a harvest of fruits and seeds for birds to enjoy in autumn. Low-growing aubretia and golden rod bring colour to the beds, against a backdrop of laurel. A variety of herbs, including lavender and thyme, releases scent into the air.

FOUNTAIN
Large pebbles at the base of the fountain serve as bathing platforms for birds.

ARBOUR
A garden seat, shaded by a trellis arbour, offers shelter from the sun.

Northern Visitor
Juniper berries are an important source of food in autumn, especially for hungry migrant birds such as redwings.

HERB BEDS
Symmetrical herb beds enhance the formal design of the terrace.

PLANTING LIST

Clockwise from bottom left

LEFT BORDER
Barberry, fig, aubretia, sunflower, olive, golden rod, sage, mulberry

FOUNTAIN BEDS
Lavender, box, marjoram, thyme

RIGHT BORDER
Mulberry, fig, juniper, aubretia, sunflower, olive, golden rod

TERRACE
Rosemary, selection of annuals

PERGOLA
Grape vine

TREES

COMMON FIG

Ficus carica

The fig is an important food in Mediterranean countries. Often grown on plantations, this small tree or shrub is also widely naturalized and favours rocky places. It bears large, lobed leaves and produces very small, inconspicuous flowers in June. Fleshy, pear-shaped fruits ripen from green to brown or purple in August.
HEIGHT 3 m. **SPREAD** 3 m.
CULTIVATION Grow in fertile, leaf-rich, moist but well-drained soil in full sun or part shade. Shelter against cold, drying winds and protect from frost.
RELATED *F. c.* 'Brown Turkey', the hardiest variety, has dark brown fruits.

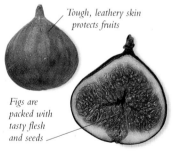

Tough, leathery skin protects fruits

Figs are packed with tasty flesh and seeds

BIRD USE Figs are eaten by jackdaws, black-headed gulls, blue tits, magpies, rooks, crows, blackbirds, sparrows, blackcaps, and other warblers.

OLIVE

Olea europaea

The olive is a small, slow-growing, evergreen tree with gnarled and twisted limbs and grey-green leaves. It grows wild in woods and dry, rocky places, and on waste land, but thrives only in a Mediterranean or similar climate. It is best known as a tree cultivated for its edible, green fruits, which ripen to black in late autumn. Small clusters of fragrant, white flowers open in May and June.
HEIGHT 10 m. **SPREAD** 8 m.
CULTIVATION Grow in deep, fertile soil that is sharply drained, in full sun. Protect from frost in colder areas.
RELATED No cultivated varieties.

Birds are attracted to olives

Slender leaves are useful nesting material

BIRD USE Fruits are eaten by gulls, black redstarts, blackbirds, tits, crows, starlings, sparrows, warblers, song thrushes, siskins, and other finches.

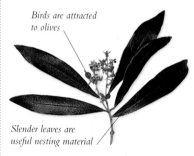

LILAC

Syringa vulgaris

Lilac is a small tree or shrub that grows wild in thickets. It is popular with gardeners for its fragrant flowers, which range in colour from white and pink to lilac and blue. It is suitable for growing in urban areas and can be used as a garden screen. Upright heads of flowers open from April to July.
HEIGHT 5 m. **SPREAD** 5 m.
CULTIVATION Grow in fertile, well-drained soil in sun. Mulch regularly. Lilac takes one or two years to become established. Hard pruning will stimulate denser growth.
RELATED *S. pubescens* subsp. *microphylla* is suitable for small gardens.

Flowers host range of insects

Small birds may nest in sparse foliage

BIRD USE Seeds are eaten by siskins and other finches. Thrushes and blackbirds may nest if the branches have been thickened by hard pruning.

SHRUBS AND CLIMBERS

BARBERRY

Berberis vulgaris

A native plant of southern and central Europe, barberry has long been cultivated for its flowers and attractive fruits. It is an evergreen shrub with finely branching twigs that bear glossy, toothed leaves and sharp spines. Barberry is suitable for hedging or a shrub border. Yellow berries ripen to orange-red in August and September.
HEIGHT 4 m. **SPREAD** 4 m.
CULTIVATION Grow in any well-drained soil in sun or part shade. Full sun produces the best autumn colours.
RELATED *B. darwinii*, an evergreen species, is particularly attractive to birds and is suitable for hedging.

Oblong berries are acid-tasting

Spiny branches protect birds from predators

BIRD USE Fruits are eaten by crows, blackbirds, fieldfares, thrushes, spotted flycatchers, tits, nuthatches, blackcaps, garden warblers, and finches.

COMMON JUNIPER

Juniperus communis

Juniper is a small, dense, evergreen shrub or tree. It grows on heaths and moors, and in woods, and is most commonly found on high ground in the southern region. Tiny, yellow flowers are borne on separate male and female plants from May to July. The male plant produces yellow cones, while the female bears fleshy, berry-like fruits that contain seeds. They ripen from green to black over 3 years.
HEIGHT 8 m. **SPREAD** 4 m.
CULTIVATION Grow in any well-drained soil in sun or part shade.
RELATED *J. c.* 'Hibernica' (*shown above*) grows about 20 cm per year.

Tightly packed needles offer good nest cover

Berries are eaten by many birds

BIRD USE Berries are eaten by great spotted woodpeckers, waxwings, thrushes, tits, treecreepers, crows, blackcaps, siskins, and other finches.

LAVENDER

Lavandula angustifolia

Lavender is a very aromatic, evergreen shrub that grows on dry, sunny sites. It is widely cultivated as an ornamental plant, and is suitable for low hedging. Lavender has a high nectar content, which makes it attractive to bees and ideal for wildflower gardens. Pale to deep purple flowers are borne from June to September, followed by small fruits each containing 4 nutlets.
HEIGHT AND SPREAD 30–60 cm.
CULTIVATION Grow in fertile, well-drained soil in full sun. Trim in spring to maintain compactness and shape.
RELATED *L. a.* 'Hidcote' (*shown above*) is compact with silvery leaves.

Birds feed on dry seedheads

Flowers attract butterflies and bees

BIRD USE Seeds are eaten by serins, goldfinches, and crossbills. Long stems and flower spikes make good nesting material.

Shrubs and Climbers

MULBERRY

Morus nigra

Mulberry is a small, deciduous shrub
or tree cultivated for its fruits and
foliage, which is used as food for
silkworms. It is commonly found
growing in woodland. Small, pale
green flowers are produced in spring,
followed by succulent, green fruits in
late summer, which ripen to purple.
HEIGHT 20 m. **SPREAD** 15 m.
CULTIVATION Grow in moderately
fertile, moist but well-drained soil in
full sun. Provide shelter from cold,
drying winds and protect from frost.
RELATED White mulberry (*M. alba,
shown below, left*) grows to 10 m high.
M. a. 'Pendula' suits small gardens.

White fruit ripens to pink and red   *Birds enjoy the juicy, fleshy fruits*

BIRD USE Fruits are eaten by tits,
waxwings, black redstarts, spotted
flycatchers, nuthatches, crows, finches,
sparrows, warblers, and woodpigeons.

FIRETHORN

Pyracantha coccinea

A close relative of cotoneaster,
firethorn is a dense, evergreen, spiny
shrub that grows in hedgerows and
thickets. It is frequently used in
gardens for covering walls or as
hedging. Profuse clusters of white
or pink flowers are borne in early
summer, followed by scarlet berries.
HEIGHT 2 m. **SPREAD** 2 m.
CULTIVATION Grow in fertile, well-
drained soil in full sun or part shade.
Where the plant is trained against a
wall, support it with wires or trellis.
Trim surplus growth in early summer.
RELATED *P.* 'Golden Dome' forms
a dense mound with yellow berries.

Spiny branches provide secure nesting sites

Leaves attract aphids and caterpillars

BIRD USE Berries are eaten by
waxwings, blackbirds, song thrushes,
starlings, and blackcaps. One blackbird
will defend and strip a single bush.

GRAPE VINE

Vitis vinifera

Grape vine is a deciduous, woody
climber that clings to supports by
means of tendrils. It is suitable for
growing over a trellis or for training
against a wall. Mainly used for making
wine, grapes are cultivated worldwide
where the climate is warm enough.
Green, scented flowers open in May
and June, followed by rounded fruits.
HEIGHT 30 m.
CULTIVATION Grow in well-drained,
fertile soil that is preferably neutral
to alkaline, in full sun or part shade.
Protect against late frost.
RELATED *V. v.* 'Purpurea' is an
ornamental vine with inedible grapes.

Fruits are enjoyed by many birds

Grapes ripen in colour according to climate

BIRD USE Fruits are eaten by collared
doves, ring-necked parakeets, green
woodpeckers, waxwings, thrushes, tits,
starlings, warblers, crows, and finches.

HERBACEOUS PLANTS

AUBRETIA
Aubrieta deltoidea

Aubretia is an evergreen perennial that forms mounds or carpets. The plant makes a colourful display when allowed to trail over rocks, banks, and walls, and is suitable for growing as ground cover or in a rock garden. Long-lasting, purple to lilac flowers are produced from March to June.
HEIGHT 5 cm. **SPREAD** to 60 cm.
CULTIVATION Grow in moderately fertile, well-drained soil that is preferably neutral or alkaline, in full sun. Cut back after flowering to maintain the plant's compactness.
RELATED *A.* x *cultorum* 'J. S. Baker' bears purple, white-eyed flowers.

Sparrows sometimes strip petals from flowers

Plump flower buds attract birds

BIRD USE House sparrows, dunnocks, warblers, and tits eat aphids and other resident insects. House sparrows and starlings take flowers for nesting.

SUNFLOWER
Helianthus annuus

Brought to Europe from the Americas for their oily seeds, sunflowers are often cultivated as a crop. They can also be seen growing wild on waste land and are very attractive to bees. Large daisy-like flowerheads are borne on tall, single stems during summer.
HEIGHT 3 m. **SPREAD** to 60 cm.
CULTIVATION Grow in moderately fertile, moist but well-drained soil that is neutral to alkaline, in full sun. Use stakes to support the flowers, which thrive in long, hot summers.
RELATED *H. a.* 'Teddy Bear' is suitable for containers. *H. salicifolius* and *H.* x *laetiflorus* suit wild gardens.

Seeds are important in birdfeed mixes

BIRD USE Sunflower seeds are eaten by collared doves, crows, waxwings, long-tailed tits, nuthatches, crossbills, bramblings, and greenfinches.

GOLDEN ROD
Solidago virgaurea

Golden rod is an herbaceous perennial that grows in verges, woods, and scrub, and on grassland. It is best suited to wild gardens since it tends to be invasive. Small, yellow daisy-like flowers grow in loose groups from July to September and are followed by heads of small, hairy seeds. Both the leaves and flowers yield a yellow dye.
HEIGHT 75 cm. **SPREAD** 45 cm.
CULTIVATION Grow in poor, preferably sandy, well-drained soil in full sun. Self-seeds easily.
RELATED *S.* 'Goldenmosa' (*shown above*) has wrinkled leaves. *S.* 'Golden Wings' thrives in poor soil.

Dense masses of tiny seeds

Golden-yellow flowers attract pollinating insects

BIRD USE Pollinating insects on the flowers are eaten by many birds. Seeds are eaten by greenfinches, goldfinches, siskins, and linnets.

ADDITIONAL PLANTS

Below are additional planting suggestions of hardy varieties that tolerate a wide range of conditions. Like the plants on the previous pages, they are not exclusive to this region, and many of them can be cultivated successfully elsewhere in Europe.

TREES

SILVER FIR

Abies alba

Silver fir is a fast-growing conifer that is often planted as a windbreak or hedge. Small, yellow male flowers cluster under twigs while tiny female flowers grow on the upper branches. The long, yellow-green cones, which ripen to brown, usually grow among the higher branches.
HEIGHT 25 m. **SPREAD** 5 m.
CULTIVATION Grow in fertile, moist, and well-drained soil in full sun, with shelter from the wind. Silver firs are shade-tolerant but dislike alkaline soil.
RELATED A dwarf variety of Pacific fir such as *A. amabilis* 'Spreading Star' is ideal for ground cover. Nikko fir (*A. homolepis*) tolerates air pollution.
BIRD USE Seeds are eaten by rooks, marsh tits, coal tits, and finches. Foliage is used for nesting.

SWEET CHESTNUT

Castanea sativa

Sweet or Spanish chestnut is a tall, deciduous tree that grows in woods. Creamy-yellow flowers with a strong scent are produced in catkins in July. Edible nuts enclosed within a prickly husk ripen in October.
HEIGHT 30 m. **SPREAD** 15 m.
CULTIVATION Grow in well-drained, fertile, preferably sandy, soil in sun or part shade. Chestnuts are suitable for coppicing (*see p. 29*).
BIRD USE Fruits are eaten by jackdaws, jays, magpies, marsh tits, blue tits, great tits, and chaffinches.

WALNUT

Juglans regia

This tall, deciduous tree with aromatic foliage is a native of southeast Europe and western Asia. The walnut was introduced to southern Europe and parts of central Europe for its edible nuts. The yellow catkins, male and female on the same tree, are borne in spring and early summer. The fleshy, green fruits ripen to brown and then split to reveal the hard-shelled nuts.
HEIGHT 30 m. **SPREAD** 20 m.
CULTIVATION Grow in fertile soil in full sun. Choose your site carefully, since walnut trees are long lived and have a life expectancy of up to 200 years. Protect young trees from frost damage, especially in early spring.
RELATED *J. r.* 'Broadview' and *J. r.* 'Buccaneer' produce reliable crops of quality nuts. Cut-leaved walnut (*J. r.* 'Laciniata') has slightly drooping branches and deeply cut leaves.
BIRD USE Nuts are eaten by great spotted woodpeckers, woodpigeons, magpies, jackdaws, coal tits, blue tits, great tits, and hawfinches.

SHRUBS AND CLIMBERS

BROOM

Cytisus scoparius

An evergreen, many-branched shrub, broom grows on open ground, usually in sandy soil. Small varieties suit rock gardens and raised beds, while larger varieties can be used in shrub borders. Broom produces a mass of bright yellow, pea-like flowers in May and June. The seeds develop in brown pods and are dispersed when ripe.
HEIGHT 2.5 m. **SPREAD** 1 m.
CULTIVATION Grow in full sun in well-drained, fertile soil and shelter from wind. Broom is tolerant of poor, acid soils but dislikes chalky soil. Propagate from seed in autumn or spring, or take cuttings in summer.

RELATED *C. demissus* is a deciduous, slow-growing, low shrub that is good for banks. *C. × spachianus* has fragrant flowers in late winter and early spring.
BIRD USE Seeds are eaten by rooks, greenfinches, and hawfinches. Flowers are eaten by waxwings.

JASMINE

Jasminum fruticans

Jasmine is an evergreen shrub or climber with angular, green stems. It is native to the Mediterranean region and grows in rocky, bushy places. Small clusters of scented, yellow flowers appear in summer, followed by shiny, black berries.
HEIGHT 1 m. **SPREAD** 50 cm.
CULTIVATION Grow in fertile, well-drained soil in full sun or part shade.
RELATED Winter jasmine (*J. nudiflorum*) flowers in winter, even on north walls, but needs shelter from wind. Common jasmine (*J. officinale*) is a vigorous, flowering climber.
BIRD USE Flowers are eaten by waxwings. Birds use the dense growth for nesting.

GARDEN PEA

Pisum sativum

A climbing annual with twining tendrils, the garden pea has been cultivated since prehistoric times but does not often grow wild in Europe. White flowers borne in summer develop into pods containing rows of plump, green seeds.
HEIGHT 2 m. **SPREAD** 1 m.
CULTIVATION Grow in rich, moist soil. Pea can be trained to grow up trellises, wigwams, and garden canes.
RELATED *P. s.* 'Coral' is a high-yielding, early-cropping variety. *P. s.* 'Carouby de Maussane' can be trained to scramble up a screen.
BIRD USE Peas are eaten by jays, woodpigeons, jackdaws, magpies, blue tits, blackcaps, siskins, linnets, crossbills, and other finches.

HERBACEOUS PLANTS

BUR-MARIGOLD

Bidens ferulifolia

This annual herb grows along the banks of ponds and streams and in areas prone to winter flooding. Its common name comes from the small, flattened fruits, or burs, which are hooked and can cling to clothing. Button-like, golden-yellow flowers open between July and October.
HEIGHT 60 cm. **SPREAD** 30 cm.
CULTIVATION Grow in well-drained soil in sun. Dead-head to prolong flowering, or leave flowers to self-seed.
RELATED *Cosmos atrosanguineus* (syn. *Bidens atrosanguinea*) is a crimson-flowered garden variety with reddish-brown stems and a chocolate scent.
BIRD USE Fruits are eaten by linnets, carrion crows, greenfinches, redpolls, and goldfinches.

FLOWERING RUSH

Butomus umbellatus

Flowering rush is an evergreen perennial that is commonly found growing in shallow water and pond margins. It produces twisting, narrow, blade-like leaves, which mature from mid-green, through bronze-purple, to dark green. Loose heads of fragrant, pink flowers are borne in succession during late summer.
HEIGHT 1 m. **SPREAD** 45 cm.
CULTIVATION Grow in water down to a depth of 25 cm, in sun. Propagate by division or by sowing seeds in spring or late summer.
BIRD USE Visiting birds are attracted by insects and use the leaves for cover.

CROCUS

Crocus biflorus

Crocuses can be found growing in woodlands, scrub, and meadows. They are ideal for naturalizing in grass. White or blue, goblet-shaped flowers are produced in early spring.
HEIGHT 10 cm. **SPREAD** 6–8 cm.
CULTIVATION Plant corms 5–6 cm deep in well-drained soil in sun.

Divide and replant clumps when they become overcrowded.
BIRD USE Flower petals are attacked by starlings and house sparrows.

CROWN IMPERIAL

Fritillaria imperialis

Crown imperials are ideal for growing in a rock garden or sunny border. They have a tall stem bearing glossy leaves and a head of up to five large, orange, bell-shaped flowers in spring.
HEIGHT 1.5 m. **SPREAD** 30 cm.
CULTIVATION Grow in fertile, well-drained soil in full sun. Support the tall, flower-bearing stems with stakes.
RELATED *F. i.* 'Lutea' has bright yellow flowers and *F. i.* 'Rubra Maxima' produces red flowers.
BIRD USE Nectar is sipped by blue tits, blackcaps, and garden warblers.

YELLOW FLAG

Iris pseudoacorus

Yellow flag grows wild over much of Europe, usually in marshes, ditches, and waterside places. It produces long, sword-shaped leaves, which form a fan, and large, yellow flowers, which appear from mid- to late summer. Note: all parts are poisonous if eaten.
HEIGHT to 2m. **SPREAD** to 60 cm.
CULTIVATION Grow as a marginal plant in damp soil in full sun or dappled shade. Increase by division in late summer or by seed in autumn.
RELATED Blue flag (*I. versicolor*) has purple, yellow-veined flowers. Orris root (*I. germanica* var. *florentina*) bears very fragrant, white flowers.
BIRD USE Leaves provide cover for birds visiting nearby water.

HONESTY

Lunaria annua

Also known as satin flower, honesty is widely grown in gardens and has become naturalized in many parts of Europe. Red-purple or white, sweet-scented flowers appear in late spring and summer and attract butterflies, moths, bees, and smaller insects. The seed pods are used for decoration.

HEIGHT 75 cm. **SPREAD** 30 cm.
CULTIVATION Grow in well-drained soil, preferably in part shade. Honesty self-seeds easily but seed may be sown in early summer.
RELATED Perennial honesty (*L. rediviva*) bears flat, oval seed pods.
BIRD USE Birds feed on visiting insects. Seeds are eaten by bullfinches.

LEMON BALM

Melissa officinalis

This herbaceous, branching perennial is grown for its lemon-scented leaves and as a decorative plant in herb gardens and borders. Balm is a native of the Mediterranean but has been introduced to central Europe, where it grows in hedges, woods, and vineyards. Spikes of small, white or pale yellow flowers, produced from June to September, attract bees.
HEIGHT 80 cm. **SPREAD** 45 cm.
CULTIVATION Sow seed in autumn or spring, in moist soil in part sun.
RELATED *M. o* 'All Gold' has golden-yellow foliage. *M. o.* 'Aurea' has gold-splashed, dark green leaves.
BIRD USE Birds feed on visiting insects. Seeds are eaten by goldfinches.

MILLET

Panicum miliaceum

Millet is grown as a crop in southern Europe, but sometimes grows wild in open grassland or wooded areas. Spikes of green flowerheads, tinted purple, emerge from a sheath of narrow leaves in late summer. Millet seeds, a common ingredient in commercial birdseed mixtures, ripen and shed themselves in early autumn.
CULTIVATION Grow in moderately fertile, well-drained soil in full sun. Sow seed in spring or divide in mid-spring or early summer.
HEIGHT 1 m. **SPREAD** 50 cm.
RELATED Italian millet or foxtail millet (*Setaria italica*) can be grown as a garden plant and produces flowers of several colours.
BIRD USE Seeds are eaten by rooks, collared doves, magpies, jackdaws, starlings, sparrows, and finches.

Chapter Six

BIRD VISITORS

A N INCREASING NUMBER of sightings of European bird species is being recorded in gardens. This finding reflects the growth of urban areas and housing developments with gardens, and the trend for birds to venture beyond their natural habitats in search of food and shelter. Crop failures and hard weather may force rare birds that usually live in remote places to visit gardens, while spring and autumn migrations are often the source of unusual bird visitors – even a fleeting glimpse of a migrating species counts as a sighting.

This chapter describes the birds that are most likely to be seen in gardens as passing visitors, regular diners, or residents. Watching birds enjoy the environment that you have created for them is the ultimate reward of a birdfeeder's garden. Keep your binoculars to hand and learn how to describe the features of an unfamiliar bird properly, so that you can learn more about its habits and preferences in a field guide or other reference book. You may be surprised at how quickly your list of bird visitors grows.

Family Fun
A family of bullfinches nesting in your garden can provide an exciting opportunity to watch the daily activities of birds.

HOW TO USE THE BIRD GUIDE

STRICTLY SPEAKING, a "garden bird" is defined as one that visits gardens regularly in search of food, water, shelter, and nesting sites. However, almost any species might be seen, including "accidental" visitors seeking refuge from bad weather or merely passing on migration, and spectacular but possibly less-welcome birds of prey, which are attracted to small birds. For most gardens, between 15 and 20 species of bird is a good range of visitors. This chapter profiles 66 birds that are likely to visit built-up areas and gardens in Europe, but not all birds will be seen in all three regions.

The profiles are organized according to the scientific classification devised by the botanist Carl von Linné. This system groups families of bird species with similar characteristics (see below). Within each family, the birds are ordered alphabetically by their Latin names. Each profile includes a portrait of the adult bird, and a distribution map showing the bird's migratory habits. Concise text outlines the bird's appearance and native habitat, and describes its common song and calls, and nesting habits. It also identifies garden features and foods that are likely to attract the bird.

BIRD FAMILIES IN LINNAEAN ORDER

Family Name	Common Name	Family Name	Common Name
Ardeidae	Grey heron	Prunellidae	Dunnock
Anatidae	Mallard	Turdidae	Robin, black redstart, redstart, blackbird, fieldfare, song thrush, redwing, mistle thrush
Accipitridae	Sparrowhawk		
Falconidae	Kestrel		
Phasianidae	Pheasant	Sylviidae	Garden warbler, blackcap, chiffchaff, goldcrest
Rallidae	Moorhen		
Laridae	Black-headed gull, common gull, herring gull	Muscicapidae	Spotted flycatcher, pied flycatcher
		Aegithalidae	Long-tailed tit
Columbidae	Street pigeon, woodpigeon, collared dove	Paridae	Marsh tit, coal tit, blue tit, great tit
		Sittidae	Nuthatch
Psittacidae	Ring-necked parakeet	Certhiidae	Treecreeper
Strigidae	Little owl, tawny owl	Corvidae	Jay, magpie, jackdaw, rook, carrion crow
Apodidae	Swift		
Upupidae	Hoopoe	Sturnidae	Starling
Picidae	Green woodpecker, great spotted woodpecker	Passeridae	House sparrow, tree sparrow
Hirundinidae	Swallow, house martin	Fringillidae	Chaffinch, brambling, serin, greenfinch, goldfinch, redpoll, siskin, linnet, crossbill, bullfinch, hawfinch
Motacillidae	Pied wagtail		
Bombycillidae	Waxwing		
Troglodytidae	Wren	Emberizidae	Reed bunting

GUIDE TO BIRD PROFILES

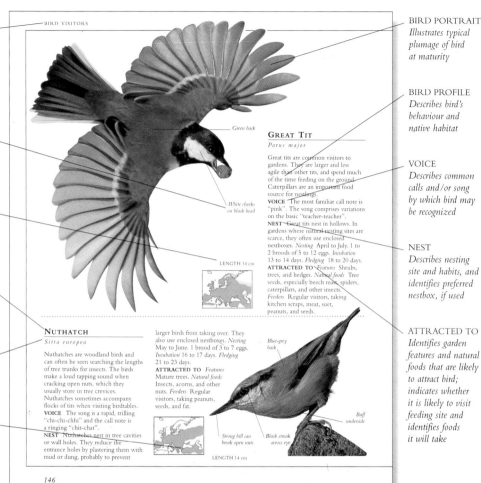

RUNNING HEAD
*Left-hand page
shows chapter title;
right-hand page shows
span of bird families
illustrated on spread*

ANNOTATION
*Highlights
distinguishing feature*

LENGTH
*Gives average
length of bird from
beak tip to tail*

COMMON NAME
*Non-scientific name
by which bird is known*

BIOLOGICAL NAME
*Scientific name by
which bird is known*

DISTRIBUTION MAP
*Shows bird's annual
migratory pattern
in Europe*

BIRD PORTRAIT
*Illustrates typical
plumage of bird
at maturity*

BIRD PROFILE
*Describes bird's
behaviour and
native habitat*

VOICE
*Describes common
calls and/or song
by which bird may
be recognized*

NEST
*Describes nesting
site and habits, and
identifies preferred
nestbox, if used*

ATTRACTED TO
*Identifies garden
features and natural
foods that are likely
to attract bird;
indicates whether
it is likely to visit
feeding site and
identifies foods
it will take*

BIRD VISITORS

Green back

*White cheeks
on black head*

LENGTH 14 cm

GREAT TIT
Parus major

Great tits are common visitors to
gardens. They are larger and less
agile than other tits, and spend much
of the time feeding on the ground.
Caterpillars are an important food
source for nestlings.
VOICE The most familiar call note is
"pink". The song comprises variations
on the basic "teacher-teacher".
NEST Great tits nest in hollows. In
gardens where natural nesting sites are
scarce, they often use enclosed
nestboxes. *Nesting* April to July. 1 to
2 broods of 5 to 12 eggs. *Incubation*
13 to 14 days. *Fledging* 18 to 20 days.
ATTRACTED TO *Features* Shrubs,
trees, and hedges. *Natural foods* Tree
seeds, especially beech mast, spiders,
caterpillars, and other insects.
Feeders Regular visitors, taking
kitchen scraps, meat, suet,
peanuts, and seeds.

NUTHATCH
Sitta europea

Nuthatches are woodland birds and
can often be seen searching the lengths
of tree trunks for insects. The birds
make a loud tapping sound when
cracking open nuts, which they
usually store in tree crevices.
Nuthatches sometimes accompany
flocks of tits when visiting birdtables.
VOICE The song is a rapid, trilling
"chi-chi-chhi" and the call note is
a ringing "chit-chat".
NEST Nuthatches nest in tree cavities
or wall holes. They reduce the
entrance holes by plastering them with
mud or dung, probably to prevent

larger birds from taking over. They
also use enclosed nestboxes. *Nesting*
May to June. 1 brood of 3 to 7 eggs.
Incubation 16 to 17 days. *Fledging*
21 to 23 days.
ATTRACTED TO *Features*
Mature trees. *Natural foods*
Insects, acorns, and other
nuts. *Feeders* Regular
visitors, taking peanuts,
seeds, and fat.

*Blue-grey
back*

*Strong bill can
break open nuts*

*Black streak
across eye*

*Buff
underside*

LENGTH 14 cm

146

HOW BIRDS ARE NAMED

Every type of bird is named according to a recognized
hierarchy of scientific groups. The most commonly
used divisions in this bird guide are explained below.

FAMILY Laridae
The family name groups
together bird species
belonging to several genera
(*see genus below*) that share
similar characteristics.

GENUS/SPECIES
Larus argentatus
The first Latin name (*Larus*)
indicates the bird's genus,

which is applied to a single
or number of closely related
species. The second Latin
name (*argentatus*) identifies
the individual species.

SUBSPECIES *Larus argentatus*
subsp. *argenteus*
This indicates a major
division within an individual
species of bird.

KEY TO DISTRIBUTION MAPS

Distribution of the birds featured in this bird guide
varies across the three regions of Europe, according
to the migratory habit of each species. Using the
distribution map, you can determine which birds
might visit your garden at different times of the year.

Winter-only resident

Summer-only resident

Year-round resident

DISTRIBUTION MAP

Distinctive hunched position

Curved neck allows head to dart forwards to catch prey

Large, broad wings

GREY HERON

Ardea cinerea

Rarely seen in gardens, herons are unmistakably large and solitary birds. They are occasionally attracted by garden ponds, and may become pests since they can remove the entire fish and frog population of a pond in a short series of visits. The birds usually make forays in the early morning.
VOICE A harsh, loud "fraank".
NEST Several herons usually nest together in a heronry at a traditional site. The most common site for the nest is at the top of a tall tree. *Nesting* February to April. 1 brood of 4 to 5 eggs. *Incubation* 25 to 26 days. *Fledging* 50 days.
ATTRACTED TO *Features* Ponds. *Natural foods* Fish, amphibians, and small mammals. *Feeders* Rare visitors, but have been known to take scraps of meat during hard weather.

LENGTH 90 cm

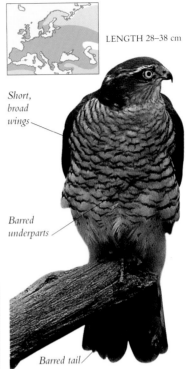

LENGTH 28–38 cm

Short, broad wings

Barred underparts

Barred tail

SPARROWHAWK

Accipiter nisus

Sparrowhawks have become increasingly common visitors to built-up areas, where they prey on small birds. They are adept at catching birds on the wing, flying low over hedges so as to take their prey by surprise. The victims are usually no bigger than blackbirds, although sparrowhawks have been known to take larger birds, such as woodpigeons or, rarely, pheasants. There is no evidence that their hunting activity adversely affects bird populations. Sparrowhawks are wary of humans and are therefore unlikely to choose gardens as nesting sites.
VOICE The call is a shrill "kek-kek" or "kew-kew".
NEST Sparrowhawks will sometimes use old pigeon nests in the forks of trees. *Nesting* May to July. 1 brood of 4 to 6 eggs. *Incubation* 39 to 42 days. *Fledging* 24 to 30 days.
ATTRACTED TO *Features* Trees. *Natural foods* Small birds. *Feeders* Visit only to prey on smaller birds.

MALLARD

Anas platyrhynchos

Mallards are the ancestors of most domestic or farmyard ducks. When the two interbreed, unusual colour variants are produced. The birds are often seen in urban areas and may visit gardens with a pond or with water nearby and plenty of cover for nesting.
VOICE Female makes a loud, harsh "quack"; male's "quack" is quieter.
NEST Mallards usually nest on the ground but may use hollow trees or duckboxes. *Nesting* March to July. 1 brood of 8 to 12 eggs. *Incubation* 27 to 28 days. *Fledging* 50 to 60 days.
ATTRACTED TO *Features* Ponds and lawns. *Natural foods* Pondlife and grass. *Feeders* Occasional visitors, taking scattered bread and grain.

LENGTH 60 cm

Bill "dabbles" in water for food

Curled tail feathers

KESTREL

Falco tinnunculus

Kestrels are the most common members of the falcon family and the only ones to make frequent visits to residential areas. They are often seen on motorway verges and even in large, open spaces within cities. The birds are easy to recognize by their habit of hovering when searching for prey. They will chase small birds and even seize them from bushes. When eating, kestrels shield or "mantle" their food to stop other birds from stealing it.
VOICE The call is "kik-kik-kik".
NEST Kestrels prefer high nesting sites, such as tree cavities or the ledges of buildings. They will sometimes settle in nests that have been abandoned by crows or use open-fronted nestboxes. *Nesting* April to July. 1 brood of 3 to 6 eggs. *Incubation* 27 to 29 days. *Fledging* 27 to 32 days.
ATTRACTED TO *Features* Trees. *Natural foods* Voles, small birds, and large insects. *Feeders* Visit only to prey on smaller birds.

Long, pointed wings

Slender tail opens to broad fan

Sharp, hooked bill for tearing flesh

LENGTH 34 cm

PHEASANT

Phasianus colchicus

Introduced to Europe by the Romans, pheasants are now common across most of the central region in Europe. Male birds are more frequent visitors to gardens than females, and can usually be seen in autumn and winter. The birds return regularly to sites with reliable sources of food and dense foliage in which to take refuge.
VOICE A loud "kork-kok" given by the male.
NEST Pheasants nest in shallow depressions on the ground beneath cover. *Nesting* March to July. 1 brood of 8 to 15 eggs. *Incubation* 23 to 28 days. *Fledging* 12 days.
ATTRACTED TO *Features* Hedges and undergrowth. *Natural foods* Buds, insects, and fruits. *Feeders* Occasional visitors, taking bread and seeds.

Males "whirr" their wings to attract females' attention

Long, barred tail

LENGTH
Male 84 cm
Female 58 cm

MOORHEN

Gallinula chloropus

Often seen in parks, moorhens visit gardens that have water nearby. When disturbed, they can run at great speed. The birds are also agile in trees, often roosting on branches, and fight battles over territory with their feet.
VOICE The call is a sharp "purruk"
NEST Moorhens either build anchored nests on water, or nest in hedges or trees. On water, they often have to add more material to the nest to keep the eggs clear of a rising water level. *Nesting* April to August. 2 or 3 broods of 5 to 8 eggs. *Incubation* 21 to 22 days. *Fledging* 40 to 50 days.
ATTRACTED TO *Features* Ponds and streams. *Natural foods* Pondlife, seeds, and berries. *Feeders* Occasional visitors, taking scattered bread and fat.

LENGTH 40 cm

Head nods when swimming

Long, slender toes are often broken in fights

COMMON GULL

Larus canus

Common gulls breed in northern Europe. They are a familiar sight along coastlines, where they can be seen foraging in shallow water. They also visit inland, usually feeding on farmland. The birds are most likely to visit gardens during winter months.
VOICE A high-pitched and shrill, laughing call.
NEST Inland, gulls nest in colonies on small islands on lakes, or they settle in trees or on buildings. They may use open nestboxes mounted high on poles. *Nesting* April to July. 1 brood of 2 to 3 eggs. *Incubation* 24 to 25 days. *Fledging* 28 days.
ATTRACTED TO *Features* Lawns and open spaces. *Natural foods* Insects, mice, worms, and berries. *Feeders* Rare visitors, taking scattered grain.

BLACK-HEADED GULL

Larus ridibundus

Best known as seabirds, black-headed gulls have become inland residents in many parts of Europe. The birds often scavenge in towns.
VOICE A harsh "kek" signals alarm. The territorial call is a raucous laugh.
NEST Small colonies settle on wasteland to nest. *Nesting* April to July. 1 brood of 3 eggs. *Incubation* 23 to 26 days. *Fledging* 35 days.
ATTRACTED TO *Features* Open spaces and lawns. *Natural foods* Insects and worms. *Feeders* Regular visitors, taking bread and kitchen scraps.

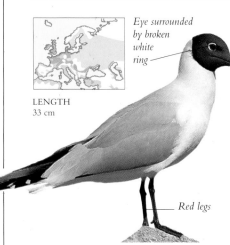

Eye surrounded by broken white ring

LENGTH 33 cm

Red legs

Head streaked brown in winter

LENGTH 38 cm

Slender bill

Green legs

HERRING GULL

Larus argentatus

Herring gulls are large, powerful, and aggressive birds with a cruising flight speed of 16 km per hour. They move inland in winter to scavenge for food in urban areas and to hunt small prey.
VOICE A harsh laugh and mewing.
NEST Herring gulls often nest on buildings. *Nesting* April to July. 1 brood of 2 to 3 eggs. *Incubation* 28 to 30 days. *Fledging* 44 to 46 days.

ATTRACTED TO *Features* Lawns and open spaces. *Natural foods* Small animals. *Feeders* Rare visitors, taking kitchen scraps on birdtables or scattered on the ground.

LENGTH 56 cm

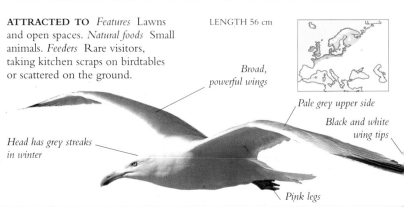

Broad, powerful wings

Pale grey upper side

Black and white wing tips

Head has grey streaks in winter

Pink legs

Wings are often barred

LENGTH 33 cm

WOODPIGEON
Columba palumbus

Frequently seen in parks and gardens, woodpigeons are more timid than street pigeons and will take flight even when approached from a distance. Large flocks of feeding woodpigeons form during autumn and winter. The birds are considered to be pests in the countryside because of their appetite for cereals, legumes, and brassicas. They can also be a nuisance in the vegetable garden.

VOICE The song is a plaintive "coo-COO-coo-coo-coo". Soft cooing can be heard during the birds' courtship.

NEST Woodpigeons usually nest in trees or, sometimes, on buildings. *Nesting* February to November. 2 broods of 2 eggs. *Incubation* 17 days. *Fledging* 20 to 35 days.

ATTRACTED TO *Features* Ponds and vegetable plots. *Natural foods* Lawn weeds, legumes, berries, and seeds. *Feeders* Rare visitors, taking kitchen scraps, grain, and other seeds.

LENGTH 40 cm

Distinctive white neck patch

White wing patch

STREET PIGEON
Columba livia

Street pigeons, commonly known as town or feral pigeons, are descendants of the rock dove and have established populations worldwide. They are a familiar sight in towns and cities and can often be seen scavenging on pavements. Street pigeons may also be seen feeding in fields alongside racing pigeons, or nesting on building ledges with neighbouring jackdaws.

VOICE A low cooing, such as "ooor-ooor" or "o-roo-coo"

NEST Street pigeons usually nest on ledges or in tree holes. They may use enclosed nestboxes. *Nesting* At any time of year in favourable conditions. 2 or 3 broods of 2 eggs. *Incubation* 17 to 18 days. *Fledging* 49 days.

ATTRACTED TO *Features* Lawns, open spaces, and cabbage patches. *Natural foods* Edible litter, and grain and other seeds. *Feeders* Regular visitors, taking scattered kitchen scraps, seeds, and breadcrumbs.

COLLARED DOVE
Streptopelia decaocto

Collared doves have always been associated with human settlements, but their spread from the southeast to most of Europe during the first half of the 20th century remains unexplained.

Distinctive black collar

VOICE The song is a monotonous "coo-COO-coo" and a double "coo".

NEST Collared doves usually nest in trees or, occasionally, on buildings. *Nesting* February to November. 3 to 6 broods of 2 eggs. *Incubation* 14 to 18 days. *Fledging* 17 days.

ATTRACTED TO *Features* Lawns and open spaces. *Natural foods* Seeds, fruits, and insects. *Feeders* Regular visitors, taking scattered grain and other seeds, bread, and kitchen scraps.

LENGTH 32 cm

Dark tail with white tip beneath

LENGTH 40 cm

Rose-pink collar

Pale green body

Male has black throat

Distinctive long tail

RING-NECKED PARAKEET

Psittacula krameri

Ring-necked parakeets are also known as rose-necked or rose-ringed parakeets. They are descendants of escaped or released cagebirds and breed in small flocks in northwestern Europe. Although these birds make attractive additions to a garden, they can be destructive when feeding and may cause serious damage to fruit trees.
VOICE A loud, screeching "kee-ak kee-ak kee-ak". Also, several quiet whistles and chattering notes.
NEST Ring-necked parakeets will sometimes enlarge and occupy holes that have been made and abandoned by woodpeckers. They may use enclosed nestboxes. *Nesting* January to June. 1 brood of 3 to 5 eggs. *Incubation* 22 days. *Fledging* 49 to 50 days.
ATTRACTED TO *Features* Orchards and large, mature gardens with fruit trees. *Natural foods* Seeds and berries. *Feeders* Regular visitors, taking fruits, nuts, kitchen scraps, and seeds.

LITTLE OWL

Athene noctua

Little owls are active mainly at night, but they often make forays at dusk too. The birds are most likely to be seen when they are hunting from perches on trees or fence-posts. When alarmed or curious, they bob up and down and can turn their heads by 180 degrees.
VOICE A plaintive "gooiek" is made by males. The call is a sharp "kiew".
NEST Little owls often nest in holes in elms or pollarded willows, or in buildings. They have been known to use rabbit holes and may use chimney or open nestboxes. *Nesting* April to July. 1 brood of 3 to 5 eggs. *Incubation* 27 to 28 days. *Fledging* 30 to 35 days.
ATTRACTED TO *Features* Large, mature trees and perches. *Natural foods* Insects, small mammals and birds, and worms. *Feeders* Never visit.

LENGTH 22 cm

Flat head

Fierce expression, with large, yellow eyes

Feathered legs

Short tail

TAWNY OWL

Strix aluco

Tawny owls are nocturnal birds that are more often heard than seen. They are one of the most common hunting birds to visit garden. Pairs of tawny owls defend their territories throughout the year.

VOICE The song is a hollow "hooo", followed by a wavering "hoo-hoo-hoo-ooooo". A sharp "ke-wick" call is used by a pair to keep in contact.

NEST Tawny owls nest in holes in trees and buildings. They may occupy the abandoned nests of squirrels or magpies, or use chimney nestboxes. *Nesting* March to June. 1 brood of 2 to 4 eggs. *Incubation* 28 to 30 days. *Fledging* 32 to 37 days.

ATTRACTED TO *Features* Large, mature trees. *Natural foods* Rodents and small birds. *Feeders* Never visit.

LENGTH 38 cm

No ear tufts

Distinctive black eyes

Rust-brown plumage with cream mottling

LENGTH 16.5 cm

Off-white throat

Short tail

Long, curved wings

HOOPOE

Upupa epops

Named after their distinctive, soft "hooping" call, which can carry over a long distance, hoopoes are found mainly in southern Europe. They are commonly seen on grassy and wooded plains, and often visit orchards, gardens, and parks. The birds can be recognized by their prominent crests, which can be raised into fans. The slender bill is used to dig out grubs and other insects from the ground.

VOICE The call is a soft, musical "hoo-hoo-hoo".

NEST Hoopoes usually nest in holes or cavities in trees, walls, or old buildings. They may use enclosed nestboxes. *Nesting* May to June. 1 brood of 8 to 10 eggs. *Incubation* 17 to 18 days. *Fledging* 28 to 30 days.

ATTRACTED TO *Features* Lawns and open spaces. *Natural foods* Grubs, worms, and large insects. *Feeders* Occasional visitors, taking mealworms scattered on the ground.

SWIFT

Apus apus

Swifts spend most of their lives in the air, even feeding and drinking as they fly. They may not land from the end of one nesting season to the start of the next in spring. When the birds are airborne at night, they drift with the wind and descend at dawn. A party of screaming swifts is a common sight on summer evenings. Being short-legged, swifts do not perch but cling to walls instead.

VOICE A screaming "sree" and chirping in the nest.

NEST Swifts often site their nests in holes in walls and under eaves, and are known for nesting inside houses. They will also use swift boxes. *Nesting* May to August. 1 brood of 2 to 3 eggs. *Incubation* 20 to 22 days. *Fledging* 35 to 49 days.

ATTRACTED TO *Features* Ponds and shrubs. *Natural foods* Flying insects such as midges swarming over water, and aphids, beetles, and flying ants. *Feeders* Never visit.

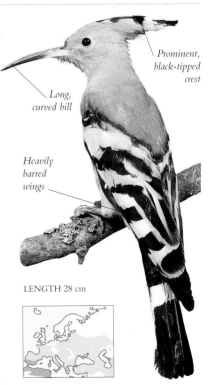

Prominent, black-tipped crest

Long, curved bill

Heavily barred wings

LENGTH 28 cm

GREEN WOODPECKER

Picus viridis

Green woodpeckers spend a lot of time on the ground, probing the soil for ants with their long tongues (up to 10 cm). Their weak bills are used for chiselling into soft wood for grubs. The birds' green plumage serves as camouflage against woodland foliage.
VOICE A loud, laughing call.
NEST Green woodpeckers excavate tree holes for nesting. They may also use enclosed nestboxes. *Nesting* April to July. 1 brood of 5 to 7 eggs. *Incubation* 18 to 19 days. *Fledging* 18 to 21 days.
ATTRACTED TO *Features* Lawns. *Natural foods* Insects. *Feeders* Rare visitors, taking fat and mealworms.

Both sexes have red crowns

Conspicuous yellow-green rump

Pale underside

LENGTH 32 cm

GREAT SPOTTED WOODPECKER

Dendrocopos major

Great spotted woodpeckers are a common sight in most wooded areas, and can be heard drumming their bills against branches in spring. Their pairs of backwards- and forwards-facing toes enable them to climb and grip on to trees with ease. Although spectacular garden visitors, the birds raid nestboxes and eat nestlings. Lesser spotted woodpeckers (*D. minor*) are the smallest woodpeckers in Europe. They can be identified by their barred backs, streaked undersides, and short bills. The birds can usually be seen in woodland and on open ground with scattered trees; they are not frequent visitors to gardens.
VOICE The call is a loud "chick". The drumming is rapid. Lesser spotted woodpeckers have a fainter but longer drumming, and a weaker call.
NEST Great spotted woodpeckers dig out tree chambers at about 3 m above ground. They may also use enclosed nestboxes. *Nesting* April to July. 1 brood of 4 to 7 eggs. *Incubation* 10 to 13 days. *Fledging* 21 days.
ATTRACTED TO *Features* Mature trees. *Natural foods* Insects. *Feeders* Regular visitors, taking peanuts.

LENGTH 23 cm

Strong bill is used to lever up bark

Prominent white shoulder patches

Red patch under tail

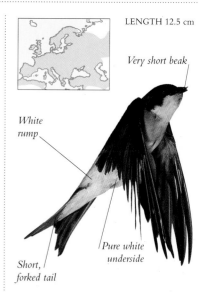

LENGTH 12.5 cm

Very short beak

White rump

Pure white underside

Short, forked tail

HOUSE MARTIN

Delichon urbica

House martins catch insects on the wing, or snatch them off the ground.
VOICE A twittery song.
NEST House martins nest under eaves or window frames, or may use bowl nests. *Nesting* May to September. 1 to 3 broods of 2 to 5 eggs. *Incubation* 15 days. *Fledging* 22 to 32 days.
ATTRACTED TO *Features* Ponds. *Natural foods* Flies, aphids, and other insects. *Feeders* Never visit.

SWALLOW

Hirundo rustica

The traditional heralds of spring, the
first swallows are likely to be seen over
reservoirs and lakes in search of an
early supply of insects. They have
been known to stay in Europe during
winter, instead of migrating to Africa.
VOICE The call is a repeated "swit-
swit-swit". The song is a pleasant,
rather quiet twittering.
NEST Swallows usually choose
beams and ledges inside buildings
as foundations for their nests. They
will also use bowl nests.

Nesting May to August. 2 to 3 broods
of 4 to 5 eggs. *Incubation* 14 to 15
days. *Fledging* 19 to 21 days.
ATTRACTED TO *Features* Ponds and
shrubs. *Natural foods* Flying insects,
from butterflies and moths to greenfly.
Feeders Never visit.

Red forehead

*Distinctive
red throat*

*Blue-black
plumage*

*Long tail
streamers*

LENGTH 18 cm

LENGTH 19 cm

*Short, stout bill
for grasping fruits*

*Wax-like
marks on
wings*

*Pink-beige
body*

Yellow tail tip

WHITE WAGTAIL

Motacilla alba subsp. *alba*

White wagtails and the closely related
pied wagtails (*M. a.* subsp. *yarrellii*) take
their name from their habit of
wagging their tails when standing still.
Both birds have adapted to living
alongside humans and can be seen
in open places near water.
VOICE A loud, sharp "chissick"
in flight, and a musical "chee-wee".
NEST Made of leaves, twigs, mosses,
and grasses, and lined with feathers,
hair, and wool. Wagtails nest in holes

in buildings and thick vegetation.
They will also use old nests of larger
birds and bird shelves. *Nesting* April
to August. 2 broods of 3 to 5 eggs.
Incubation 13 days. *Fledging* 14 days.
ATTRACTED TO *Features* Ponds and
lawns. *Natural foods* Insects. *Feeders*
Occasional visitors, taking small seeds
and crumbs scattered on the ground.

*Pale grey back distinguishes
white from pied wagtails,
which have black backs*

*Black
chest*

LENGTH 18 cm

WAXWING

Bombycilla garrulus

Native to northern Europe, waxwings
sometimes migrate to western Europe
in winter. Occasional irruptions
(sudden invasions of birds), are seen
when the annual crop of rowan berries
fails in forests in northern Europe.
The birds are specialist fruit-eaters.
When engaged in feeding on berry-
laden hedges and bushes, waxwings
show little fear of onlookers. They are
often seen in gardens and on roadsides.
VOICE The call is a trilling "shree".
NEST Waxwings conceal their
nests among the dense foliage of
coniferous trees, at between 3 m and
15 m above the ground. *Nesting* June
to September. 1 brood of 5 to 6 eggs.
Incubation 14 to 15 days. *Fledging*
14 to 17 days.
ATTRACTED TO *Features* Trees,
hedges, and shrubs. *Natural foods*
Rowan and hawthorn berries and
other fruits, and insects. *Feeders*
Occasional visitors, taking fruits
during hard weather.

WREN

Troglodytes troglodytes

Wrens are small, secretive birds with powerful voices. They feed on the ground, but tend to keep near cover.
VOICE A loud, trilling song is heard most of the year. Calls include a hard "tick-tick-tick" and a rolling "churr".
NEST Wrens nest in holes in banks, walls, and trees. They may also use open nestboxes. *Nesting* April to July. 2 broods of 5 to 6 eggs. *Incubation* 14 to 15 days. *Fledging* 16 to 17 days.

LENGTH 9.5 cm

ATTRACTED TO *Features* Climbers, dense foliage, and undergrowth. *Natural foods* Grubs and spiders. *Feeders* Rare visitors, taking scattered breadcrumbs and grated cheese.

Barred rust-brown back

Short tail, often cocked

LENGTH 14.5 cm

Streaked plumage

Slim bill for eating insects

DUNNOCK

Prunella modularis

Dunnocks, formerly known as hedge sparrows, have shy, skulking habits, and interesting social lives. Rather than keeping in simple, monogamous pairs of male and female, they form groups of one male with two females, or two males with one female, or two of each. Male birds quiver their wings to warn off rivals and intruders.
VOICE Warbling phrases lasting for four to five seconds. A shrill "tseep" keeps a group in contact.
NEST Dunnocks nest in shrubs and thick undergrowth. *Nesting* April to August. 2 to 3 broods of 4 to 5 eggs. *Incubation* 14 days. *Fledging* 12 days.
ATTRACTED TO *Features* Hedges, shrubs, and dense cover. *Natural foods* Seeds and insects. *Feeders* Occasional visitors, taking scattered crumbs.

ROBIN

Erithacus rubecula

Robins are tame garden visitors in Britain but, elsewhere in Europe, they are known as shy woodland birds. Robins defend their territories aggressively for most of the year.
VOICE A liquid warbling. The alarm call is "tseeee" and a repeated "tic".
NEST Robins will nest in holes in trees, among dense climbers, or in wall recesses. They sometimes use letterboxes or discarded items such as old tins. *Nesting* April to July. 2 broods of 5 to 6 eggs.

LENGTH 14 cm

Incubation 14 days.
Fledging 13 to 14 days.
ATTRACTED TO *Features* Hedges, shrubs, dense foliage, and undergrowth. *Natural foods* Insects, snails, worms, spiders, and fruits. *Feeders* Regular visitors, taking peanuts, kitchen scraps, pastry, mealworms, grain, and other seeds.

Red face

Pale feathers under tail

Red breast

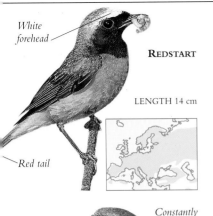

White forehead

REDSTART

LENGTH 14 cm

Red tail

Constantly quivering tail

Black or grey chest

LENGTH 14 cm

BLACK REDSTART

REDSTART/ BLACK REDSTART

Phoenicurus spp.

Although redstarts (*P. phoenicurus*) can easily be distinguished from black redstarts (*P. ochruros*), both birds share similar habits. They display restless behaviour when searching for insects. Redstarts favour woodlands, while black redstarts prefer cliffs, quarries, and buildings.
VOICE The alarm call is "sip"; other calls are a long "wheet" and "whee-tick-tick". The song consists of stuttering phrases, like jangling keys.
NEST Both species nest in holes in trees or buildings and may use enclosed nestboxes. *Nesting* May to June. 2 to 3 broods of 4 to 6 eggs. *Incubation* 13 to 17 days. *Fledging* 12 to 19 days.
ATTRACTED TO *Features* Redstarts like trees; black redstarts prefer open spaces. *Natural foods* Insects. *Feeders* Redstarts never visit; black redstarts visit rarely and may take scraps.

BLACKBIRD

Turdus merula

Originally found in woodlands, blackbirds are now successful garden residents. Like thrushes, the birds have a common habit of tilting their heads to one side to listen to worms.
VOICE The song consists of fruity phrases, often ending with a chuckle. The calls include "pook-pook", a thin "seee" of warning, and a rattling alarm.
NEST Blackbirds nest in trees and may also reuse old nests. *Nesting* March to June. 2 to 3 broods of 3 to 5 eggs. *Incubation* 13 days. *Fledging* 13 to 14 days.
ATTRACTED TO *Features* Lawns, flowerbeds, and fruiting shrubs, such as cotoneaster and barberry. *Natural foods* Earthworms, insects, and fruits. *Feeders* Regular visitors, taking fruits, breadcrumbs, fat, kitchen scraps, and seeds.

Orange-ringed eye

Black plumage on males; dark brown plumage on females

LENGTH 25 cm

LENGTH 25 cm

Blue-grey head

Brown back

Speckled chest

Grey rump

Black tail

FIELDFARE

Turdus pilaris

Fieldfares are some of the noisiest members of the thrush family. The species is native to northern Europe, but is spreading south through the rest of Europe. In Scandinavia, fieldfares frequently nest in gardens and avenues. The birds aggressively defend their nesting sites by "divebombing" intruders. In winter, fieldfares roam around the countryside in flocks to feed and roost. They may come into gardens to feed on berries and other fruits in cold weather.
VOICE Chuckles and whistles interspersed with "chacks". The call is a harsh "chack-chack-chack".
NEST Fieldfares usually nest in trees or bushes, and will sometimes build nests on the ground. Several pairs of birds often nest close to each other. *Nesting* April to May. 1 to 2 broods of 4 to 6 eggs. *Incubation* 13 to 14 days. *Fledging* 14 days.
ATTRACTED TO *Features* Fruiting trees and shrubs, such as rowan, hawthorn, and holly. *Natural foods* Earthworms, snails, and fruits. *Feeders* Occasional visitors, taking windfall apples and other rotten fruits on the ground.

SONG THRUSH
Turdus philomelos

The loud, clear song of song thrushes can be heard almost all year round in the garden. When food is hard to find in dry weather, song thrushes use a unique skill to extract flesh from snail shells, repeatedly hitting a shell against a stone until it smashes.
VOICE The song consists of repeated fluting phrases. A "tick" note is made during flight.
NEST Song thrushes nest in low, well-shaded sites. The same nest may be used again for further broods. *Nesting* February to August. 2 to 3 broods of 4 to 6 eggs. *Incubation* 13 to 14 days. *Fledging* 26 to 28 days.
ATTRACTED TO *Features* Trees and shrubs. *Natural foods* Insects, worms, and fruits. *Feeders* Rare visitors, taking fat, sultanas, kitchen scraps, and windfall apples.

Cream stripe over eye

Dark brown back

Striped underside

LENGTH 21.5 cm

REDWING
Turdus iliacus

A northern European species, redwings are common visitors to gardens in Scandinavia. During winter, the birds fly down into the rest of Europe and may even be seen in city gardens in hard weather.
VOICE The call note is "tsee-ip", which sounds like chattering from a flock. The song is a repeated "cher-cher-cher".
NEST Redwings nest in shrubs, hedges, trees, or on the ground. *Nesting* May to July. 2 broods of 5 to 6 eggs. *Incubation* 14 to 15 days. *Fledging* 11 to 14 days.
ATTRACTED TO *Features* Hedges and shrubs. *Natural foods* Hawthorn berries and other fruits. *Feeders* Occasional visitors, taking fruits and kitchen scraps on the ground.

Pale brown back

Brown-spotted breast

LENGTH 23 cm

MISTLE THRUSH
Turdus viscivorus

Named after their fondness for eating mistletoe berries, mistle thrushes are the largest members of the European thrush family. They are also known as "storm cocks" because of their habit of singing from high perches in rough weather. The birds tend to be aggressive towards predators and humans that approach their nests. During harsh weather when food is short, mistle thrushes often fiercely defend trees or shrubs to prevent other birds from reaching the fruits.
VOICE The song is made up of loud, ringing variations of "tee-tor-tee-tor-tee". A harsh, rattling call is a sign of alarm.
NEST Mistle thrushes nest high in the forks of trees or on buildings. They may use the same nest or site several times. *Nesting* February to July. 2 broods of 4 eggs. *Incubation* 12 to 15 days. *Fledging* 12 to 15 days.
ATTRACTED TO *Features* Hedges and shrubs. *Natural foods* Insects, holly and yew berries, and other fruits. *Feeders* Regular visitors, taking kitchen scraps, bread, and apples.

LENGTH 27 cm

Strong bill

Pale-edged wing feathers

Boldly spotted breast

White-tipped tail feathers

LENGTH 14 cm

Rounded, plain brown head

Pale brown back

Short, thick bill

GARDEN WARBLER

Sylvia borin

In summer, garden warblers often settle in large gardens. The birds can be difficult to observe because they prefer dense cover, but their presence can be detected by their call and song.
VOICE The call note is a hard "tack-tack". The song is persistent and less varied than the song of blackcaps.
NEST Garden warblers nest in low undergrowth. *Nesting* May to July. 1 brood of 4 to 6 eggs. *Incubation* 11 to 12 days. *Fledging* 10 days.
ATTRACTED TO *Features* Shrubs and hedges. *Natural foods* Fruits. *Feeders* Rare visitors, taking scraps.

BLACKCAP

Sylvia atricapilla

Blackcaps winter mainly in the Mediterranean region. Although the birds are usually insect-eaters, they build up their body reserves with autumn fruits.
VOICE A mellow, powerful song. The alarm call is a mechanical "tack".
NEST Blackcaps suspend their nests by "handles" in bushes or among brambles or nettles. *Nesting* April to July. 1 to 2 broods of 5 eggs. *Incubation* 10 to 11 days. *Fledging* 10 to 13 days.
ATTRACTED TO *Features* Trees and bushes. *Natural foods* Seeds and fruits. *Feeders* Regular visitors, taking scraps.

Distinctive black crown

LENGTH 14 cm

Tail frequently dipped

Short wings

Dull olive-green back

LENGTH 10.5 cm

CHIFFCHAFF

Phylloscopus collybita

Chiffchaffs are most likely to be seen searching among foliage for insects when migrating in spring and autumn.
VOICE The chiffchaff's song is made up of a medley of "chiff-chaff" notes.
NEST Chiffchaffs nest at about 30 cm high in undergrowth or brambles. *Nesting* April to July. 1 brood of 6 eggs. *Incubation* 13 days. *Fledging* 14 days.
ATTRACTED TO *Features* Mature trees and shrubs. *Natural foods* Insects. *Feeders* Occasional visitors during cold weather, taking kitchen scraps.

Crown feathers are spread in display

Double wing bar

Pale underside

LENGTH 9 cm

GOLDCREST

Regulus regulus

Goldcrests tend to be secretive. They are easiest to watch in winter, when they often feed with flocks of tits.
VOICE The call is a thin "see-see" The song is a thin, twittering "tweedly-tweedly-twiddledidee".
NEST Goldcrests nest in conifers, ivy, and gorse. *Nesting* April to July. 2 broods of 7 to 10 eggs. *Incubation* 14 to 17 days. *Fledging* 16 to 20 days.
ATTRACTED TO *Features* Trees. *Natural foods* Insects. *Feeders* Rare visitors, taking cake and bread crumbs, fat, and grated cheese.

Distinctive, upright perching position

Pale-edged wing feathers

Very short legs

LENGTH 14.5 cm

PIED FLYCATCHER
Ficedula hypoleuca

Unlike other flycatchers, pied flycatchers do not return to the same perches after capturing flying insects. They are most commonly seen in woodlands, but migrant birds will visit large gardens. Pied flycatchers wag their tails constantly, and the male bird has the distinctive habit of briefly lifting one wing when perching.

Broad, white wing bars

LENGTH 13 cm

VOICE The song is simply "tchee-tchee-tchee-cher-cher".
NEST Pied flycatchers build their nests high in tree holes and wall cavities, or on building ledges. They often use enclosed nestboxes. *Nesting* May to June. 1 brood of 5 to 8 eggs. *Incubation* 13 days. *Fledging* 14 to 17 days.
ATTRACTED TO *Features* Trees and orchards. *Natural foods* Greenfly, bees, and other flying insects. *Feeders* Occasional visitors, taking scraps.

SPOTTED FLYCATCHER
Muscicapa striata

Spotted flycatchers are small, brown birds that can easily be recognized by their acrobatic chases after winged insects. After capturing food, the birds usually return to the same hunting perches. If the weather is cold, spotted flycatchers may have to rely on insects plucked from leaves or the ground.
VOICE A simple, squeaky song, a thin "zee", or a loud "tuck-tuck".
NEST Spotted flycatchers build their nests against the trunks of trees, amid dense creepers, or sometimes in masonry such as old walls. They are known to use open-fronted nestboxes. *Nesting* May to June. 1 to 2 broods of 4 to 5 eggs. *Incubation* 12 to 13 days. *Fledging* 12 to 13 days.
ATTRACTED TO *Features* Trees, shrubs, and hunting perches. *Natural foods* Bees, butterflies, and other flying insects. *Feeders* Never visit.

LONG-TAILED TIT
Aegithalos caudatus

Long-tailed tits are often encountered in family parties, as parent birds and offspring search together through shrubs for caterpillars and other small insects. To keep warm on cold nights, a flock of long-tailed tits may huddle together in

Black-striped head

Pink patches on body

9-cm long tail

thorn bushes, with each bird forming a ball of feathers. These winter parties, which also look for food together, disband at nesting time.
VOICE A shrill, mouse-like "zee-zee-zee" with a distinctive "zupp" call.
NEST Long-tailed tits usually site their nests in the forks of trees or bushes, although sometimes they will hang them in brambles. *Nesting* May to June. 1 brood of up to 12 eggs. *Incubation* 13 to 16 days. *Fledging* 14 to 18 days.
ATTRACTED TO *Features* Hedges, dense undergrowth, and overgrown gardens. *Natural foods* Insects and seeds. *Feeders* Regular visitors, taking fat smeared across tree trunks, and meat, peanuts, and grated cheese.

LENGTH 14 cm

MARSH TIT
Parus palustris

Marsh tits are small, sleek, and neat birds, which are often inquisitive and tame. They are usually encountered in pairs, foraging with other members of the tit family. Marsh tits prefer to search for food in the lower levels of vegetation and on the ground. They often hoard supplies for when food is scarce.
VOICE "Tschuppi-tschuppi-tschuppi" is often sung high in a tree. The call notes comprise "pitchu" and a scolding "tzee"

NEST Marsh tits nest in tree holes or stumps. They may use enclosed nestboxes. *Nesting* April to June. 1 to 2 broods of 7 to 10 eggs. *Incubation* 13 to 15 days. *Fledging* 17 to 20 days.
ATTRACTED TO *Features* Trees, hedges, and undergrowth. *Natural foods* Insects. *Feeders* Regular visitors, taking peanuts and scraps.

Glossy black crown

Plain brown wings

LENGTH 11.5 cm

COAL TIT
Parus ater

Coal tits are most commonly seen among conifers. The birds have unusually long toes, which enable them to grip on to bunches of conifer needles. Coal tits become frequent visitors to suburban gardens when food is scarce. They often take supplies of food from birdtables or peanut feeders and hoard them to eat later in the season.

VOICE The song is a high-pitched "cher-tee cher-tee". The call note of "zee" is similar to that of goldcrests.
NEST Coal tits nest on the ground or in low tree hollows. They may use enclosed nestboxes. *Nesting* April to June. 1 brood of 7 to 12 eggs. *Incubation* 18 days. *Fledging* 16 days.
ATTRACTED TO *Features* Trees, especially conifers. *Natural foods* Insects, nuts, and cone seeds. *Feeders* Regular visitors, taking peanuts, seeds, and fat.

White on back of head

Slender bill can carry a whole peanut

Large, white cheeks

White wing bars

LENGTH 11.5 cm

BLUE TIT
Parus caeruleus

Blue tits can easily be recognized by their acrobatic behaviour. Those that stay in towns tend to live longer than blue tits in rural areas but raise fewer young because caterpillars are scarce.
VOICE The call is a thin "tsee-tsee". The song is "tsee-tsee-tsu-hu-hu-hu-hu". "Tsee" or "chur" signals alarm.
NEST Blue tits nest in holes and will use enclosed nestboxes. *Nesting* March to June. 1 to 2 broods of 5 to 12 eggs. *Incubation* 14 days. *Fledging* 18 days.
ATTRACTED TO *Features* Shrubs and deciduous trees. *Natural foods* Insects, seeds, especially beech mast, and nectar. *Feeders* Regular visitors, taking peanuts, fruits, fat, seeds, and kitchen scraps.

Blue tail

Bright blue crown

Black stripe across eye

LENGTH 11.5 cm

Green back

White cheeks
on black head

LENGTH 14 cm

GREAT TIT

Parus major

Great tits are common visitors to
gardens. They are larger and less
agile than other tits, and spend much
of the time feeding on the ground.
Caterpillars are an important food
source for nestlings.
VOICE The most familiar call note is
"pink". The song comprises variations
on the basic "teacher-teacher".
NEST Great tits nest in hollows. In
gardens where natural nesting sites are
scarce, they often use enclosed
nestboxes. *Nesting* April to July. 1 to
2 broods of 5 to 12 eggs. *Incubation*
13 to 14 days. *Fledging* 18 to 20 days.
ATTRACTED TO *Features* Shrubs,
trees, and hedges. *Natural foods* Tree
seeds, especially beech mast, spiders,
caterpillars, and other insects.
Feeders Regular visitors, taking
kitchen scraps, meat, suet,
peanuts, and seeds.

NUTHATCH

Sitta europea

Nuthatches are woodland birds and
can often be seen searching the lengths
of tree trunks for insects. The birds
make a loud tapping sound when
cracking open nuts, which they
usually store in tree crevices.
Nuthatches sometimes accompany
flocks of tits when visiting birdtables.
VOICE The song is a rapid, trilling
"chi-chi-chhi" and the call note is
a ringing "chit-chat".
NEST Nuthatches nest in tree cavities
or wall holes. They reduce the
entrance holes by plastering them with
mud or dung, probably to prevent

larger birds from taking over. They
also use enclosed nestboxes. *Nesting*
May to June. 1 brood of 3 to 7 eggs.
Incubation 16 to 17 days. *Fledging*
21 to 23 days.
ATTRACTED TO *Features*
Mature trees. *Natural foods*
Insects, acorns, and other
nuts. *Feeders* Regular
visitors, taking peanuts,
seeds, and fat.

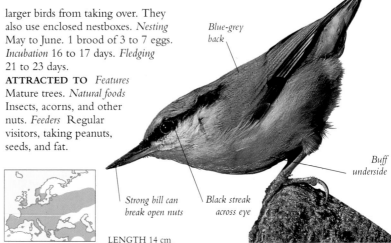

Blue-grey
back

Buff
underside

Strong bill can
break open nuts

Black streak
across eye

LENGTH 14 cm

Tweezer-like bill

White underside

Mottled-brown back

Spiny tail helps balance

LENGTH 12.5 cm

TREECREEPER
Certhia familiaris

Unlike other birds that search trees for food, treecreepers do not hang head-down but instead hop upwards, using their strong, spiny tails as props. They are woodland birds, whereas short-toed treecreepers (*C. brachydactyla*) are more likely to be seen in gardens and parks than in woods.
VOICE The song is a succession of thin, hissing notes ending in a flourish. The "see" and "sit" call notes are difficult to hear.
NEST Treecreepers nest between the cladding of buildings or in dense vegetation. They also use treecreeper nestboxes. *Nesting* April to June. 1 to 2 broods of 5 to 7 eggs. *Incubation* 14 to 15 days. *Fledging* 14 to 15 days.
ATTRACTED TO *Features* Mature trees. *Natural foods* Insects and spiders. *Feeders* Occasional visitors, sometimes taking fat or a mixture of chopped nuts and porridge, both smeared over tree bark or pressed into tree holes.

Black and white body

Long, glossy green tail

LENGTH 34 cm

JAY
Garrulus glandarius

Although shy and cautious, jays are regular visitors to rural and suburban gardens, especially in the early morning. The birds often bury any surplus food until it is needed. They are even able to retrieve their hoards when a site has been hidden under a cover of snow.
VOICE A rasping "krar" alarm and social call. Several quieter gutteral and warbling notes. Jays are good mimics.
NEST Jays usually nest in trees or tall shrubs. They also use open nestboxes. *Nesting* May to June. 1 brood of 3 to 7 eggs. *Incubation* 16 to 17 days. *Fledging* 21 to 23 days.
ATTRACTED TO *Features* Mature trees. *Natural foods* Acorns and other nuts, seeds, fruits, insects, and small mammals. *Feeders* Regular visitors, taking vegetable scraps but may also try to take peanuts from feeders.

Blue patch on top of wing

White rump revealed in flight

LENGTH 46 cm

MAGPIE
Pica pica

The nest-robbing habits of magpies make them unpopular visitors to gardens. In fact, their own nests are frequently robbed by crows. Magpies have a weak flight, but their long, tapering tails enable them to evade or make sudden attacks. They are usually seen in pairs, but tend to move in greater numbers during winter.
VOICE A harsh "kyack" or a repeated "shak-shak-shak" of alarm is often the first sign of a magpie's presence. The song is a soft warble with imitations of other birds.
NEST Magpies nest in trees or tall shrubs, or on buildings and electricity pylons. N*esting* March to May. 1 to 2 broods of 5 to 7 eggs. *Incubation* 22 days. *Fledging* 22 to 27 days.
ATTRACTED TO *Features* Trees, shrubs, and hedges. *Natural foods* Seeds, fruits, snails, slugs, spiders, and carrion. *Feeders* Regular visitors, taking bread and meat.

JACKDAW

Corvus monedula

Jackdaws are sociable, confident, and entertaining birds that have adapted easily to urban life. They are less shy than other members of the crow family and will often take up residence in gardens. Jackdaws usually live in flocks and pair up with a mate for life.
VOICE The song is a medley of "tchaks" (from which the jackdaw takes its name) and other notes. A "chaair" is often given in flight.
NEST Jackdaws nest in tree hollows or in buildings, including chimney pots. They also use enclosed nestboxes. *Nesting* April to June. 1 brood of 4 to 5 eggs. *Incubation* 17 to 18 days. *Fledging* 30 to 35 days.
ATTRACTED TO *Features* Trees and lawns. *Natural foods* Grain, fruits, insects, and eggs of other birds. *Feeders* Regular visitors, taking fruits, meat, bones, and scraps.

Grey nape

White eye ring

Dull black body

LENGTH 33 cm

ROOK

Corvus frugilegus

Rooks are sociable members of the crow family. They live in large flocks in the countryside, where they feed on worms, seeds, and grain. Rooks are regular visitors to towns, and can often be seen scouring refuse sites for food. Their tapering bills can probe deep into soil for worms and larvae.
VOICE A raucous "kaah" and various soft caws and cackles.
NEST Rooks nest in noisy colonies at the tops of tall trees. *Nesting* February to June. 1 brood of 3 to 5 eggs. *Incubation* 16 to 18 days. *Fledging* 32 to 33 days.
ATTRACTED TO *Features* Trees and lawns. *Natural foods* Seeds, nuts, earthworms, insects, and carrion. *Feeders* Regular visitors, feeding on hanging bones, bread, and fat.

Bare face patch on adults

LENGTH 46 cm

Glossy purple back

Loose thigh feathers

CARRION CROW

Corvus corone

Adult carrion crows live in territorial pairs in a variety of habitats, while their non-breeding young gather in flocks. In coastal areas, they sometimes crack open shellfish and eat them. Crows are shy of people and will approach only when they feel safe. The hooded crow (*Corvus corone cornix*), distinguished by its grey body, is a common sight in northern and western Europe.
VOICE An angry "ark-ark" is made in disputes, and "kaaaaar" signals alarm. The song is "kraa-kraa-kraa".
NEST Carrion crows nest in tree forks. *Nesting* March to June. 1 brood of 4 to 5 eggs.

Incubation 17 to 19 days. *Fledging* 32 to 36 days.
ATTRACTED TO *Features* Trees and lawns. *Natural foods* Grain, insects, nuts, and carrion. *Feeders* Regular visitors, taking bread, meat, and scraps.

Black body with green gloss

Feathered base of bill

LENGTH 47 cm

Purple-green back

STARLING
Sturnus vulgaris

Starlings are easy birds to observe because they are so bold. However, they can be a nuisance when they visit birdtables in flocks and quickly devour the food that is intended for smaller and shyer birds.

VOICE The song is a medley of notes and rattles, often with mimicked notes of other species. The calls include a harsh, screaming distress call and an aggressive "chacker-chacker"

NEST Starlings nest in buildings or tree hollows and may use enclosed nestboxes. The male may decorate the nest with leaves and flower petals. *Nesting* April to July. 1 to 2 broods of 4 to 5 eggs. *Incubation* 12 days. *Fledging* 21 days.

ATTRACTED TO *Features* Lawns. *Natural foods* Worms and insects. *Feeders* Regular visitors, taking bread, scraps, and hanging bones.

Breast spotted white in winter

Short tail

LENGTH 22 cm

Chestnut crown

LENGTH 14 cm

Black spot on white cheek

Double wing bar

HOUSE SPARROW
Passer domesticus

House sparrows were originally seed-eating birds, but they have gradually adopted new feeding habits. Their ability to exploit human environments has enabled them to spread worldwide. They are a common sight in cities, where their plumage is usually more drab than that of rural dwellers. They often capture moths that have been drawn to outdoor lamps, and will even search car radiators for insects.

VOICE The song is a medley of calls, such as "cheep" and "chirp".

LENGTH 14.5 cm

NEST House sparrows nest in holes or crevices in buildings, or in trees and hedges. They will also use vacant house-martin or swallow nests and enclosed nestboxes. After nesting, pairs use their nests as snug roosts during winter. *Nesting* March to September. 2 to 4 broods of 3 to 5 eggs. *Incubation* 14 days. *Fledging* 15 days.

ATTRACTED TO *Features* Shrubs. *Natural foods* Seeds, buds, and insects. *Feeders* Regular visitors, taking bread and seeds.

Grey crown

Short, seed-eating bill

Single wing bar

TREE SPARROW
Passer montanus

Tree sparrows are usually seen in open woodland, on river banks, and in areas with scattered trees. They are shy birds that feed on the ground, but may visit rural and suburban gardens, especially in eastern Europe. Tree sparrows can be distinguished from house sparrows by their chestnut crowns and smaller sizes. It is not known why colonies of tree sparrows often form in one area but then disappear.

VOICE The call is a metallic and finch-like "tsooit" or a distinct "tet" or "chip". The song is a repeated series of the call notes.

NEST Tree sparrows nest in tree holes, banks, thatch, and buildings. They will also occupy the disused nests of larger birds or use enclosed nestboxes. *Nesting* April to August. 2 to 3 broods of 4 to 6 eggs. *Incubation* 12 to 14 days. *Fledging* 12 to 14 days.

ATTRACTED TO *Features* Trees and shrubs. *Natural foods* Seeds. *Feeders* Regular visitors, especially during cold weather, taking seeds and kitchen scraps.

CHAFFINCH

Fringilla coelebs

Chaffinches are woodland birds that frequent trees and hedges in gardens. They feed on the ground more than other finches and form flocks in winter. They are likely to use birdtables where house sparrows are scarce. The male sets up a territory around a tree from which it can sing.
VOICE The song is a descending rattle, ending with a flourish. The common call is "pink-pink".
NEST Chaffinches nest in tree forks, hedges, or bushes. *Nesting* May to August. 1 or 2 broods of 3 to 5 eggs. *Incubation* 12 to 14 days. *Fledging* 12 to 14 days.
ATTRACTED TO *Features* Lawns and songposts in tall trees. *Natural foods* Beech mast and other seeds, weeds, caterpillars, and spiders. *Feeders* Regular visitors, taking scattered seeds and kitchen scraps.

Slate-blue head and nape on male

LENGTH 15 cm

Green rump

White-sided tail

White shoulder patch

Pink underside

BRAMBLING

Fringilla montifringilla

Bramblings are very similar in appearance to chaffinches, but can be distinguished by their distinctive orange shoulders and white rumps. The birds are often seen feeding among flocks of chaffinch. In winter, flocks of bramblings move westwards from their homeland in northern and eastern Europe.
VOICE The song, a monotonous wheeze, sounds similar to that of greenfinches. The call notes include a rasping "zweee".
NEST Bramblings usually build their nests high above the ground in tree forks. *Nesting* May to July. 1 brood of 5 to 7 eggs. *Incubation* 12 days. *Fledging* 13 to 14 days.
ATTRACTED TO *Features* Trees, especially beech and hornbeam. *Natural foods* Beech mast and other seeds. *Feeders* Rare visitors, taking scattered seeds or, sometimes, peanuts.

Male has black head in summer

Pale orange breast

White-sided tail

LENGTH 15 cm

SERIN

Serinus serinus

Serins have spread northwards through Europe over the last 100 years.
VOICE A high-pitched, jangling song, and calls of "tirrillilit" and "titteree".
NEST Serins nest in bushes or trees. *Nesting* April to July. 2 or 3 broods of 3 to 5 eggs. *Incubation* 12 to 13 days. *Fledging* 15 days.
ATTRACTED TO *Features* Perches and trees. *Natural foods* Seeds. *Feeders* Occasional visitors, taking seeds.

Dark-streaked chest

LENGTH 12 cm

Yellow rump

Yellow-green streaks on body

GREENFINCH

Carduelis chloris

Small flocks of greenfinches are becoming a common sight at birdtables in winter. Flocks may even settle to nest where seeds and peanuts are in steady supply throughout the summer. Male greenfinches have a distinctive, "fluttering" display flight.
VOICE The song is a medley of notes ending in a wheeze. The most frequent calls are a harsh "swee" and repeated "chi-chi-chi" flight note.
NEST Greenfinches build their nests in hedges and bushes. They often nest together to form a colony of up to six pairs of birds. *Nesting* April to August. 2 to 3 broods of 4 to 6 eggs. *Incubation* 12 to 14 days. *Fledging* 13 to 16 days.
ATTRACTED TO *Features* Trees, shrubs, hedges, and undergrowth. *Natural foods* Grain and seeds, including those of dandelion, elm, yew, bramble, and burdock. *Feeders* Regular visitors, taking peanuts and sunflower seeds.

Stout, pink bill

Plain green body

Yellow-streaked tail

Bright yellow wing patches

LENGTH 14.5 cm

Yellow and black wings

Red face

LENGTH 12 cm

GOLDFINCH

Carduelis carduelis

Goldfinches are likely to visit gardens that offer a supply of thistles, dandelions, groundsel, and other seed-bearing weeds. Their slender bills are designed for extracting tiny seeds, including those of teasel, which are hidden in narrow tubes and cones. Goldfinches can be recognized by their distinctive "dancing" flight.
VOICE The song is a rapid, tinkling "tsswitt-witt-witt". The call note is a shrill "pee-uu".
NEST Goldfinches often site their nests at the ends of high, horizontal branches that are hidden by leaves, or in fruit trees and thick hedges. *Nesting* April to August. 2 to 3 broods of 4 to 6 eggs. *Incubation* 11 to 13 days. *Fledging* 13 to 16 days.
ATTRACTED TO *Features* Orchards, fruit, elm, birch, and pine trees, and seeding herbs, such as lavender, lemon balm, and evening primrose. *Natural foods* Seeds. *Feeders* Occasional visitors, taking peanuts and cage-bird seeds, such as millet.

REDPOLL

Carduelis flammea

A northern European species, redpolls appear in much of western and central Europe in winter. They can be seen hanging acrobatically from branches as they extract seeds and catch small insects.
VOICE A chattering call, which is made during flight, and a nasal "sowee". The song is a mixture of the calls with added trills.
NEST Redpolls nest in shrubs or trees, or sometimes on the ground. *Nesting* May to July. 1 to 2 broods of 4 to 6 eggs. *Incubation* 10 to 12 days. *Fledging* 9 to 14 days.
ATTRACTED TO *Features* Herb beds, shrubs, and coniferous and birch trees. *Natural foods* Seeds and insects. *Feeders* Occasional visitors, taking seeds.

Buff bar on wing

Red forehead

Black chin

LENGTH 13 cm

Black cap on male

Black and yellow wing bars

Yellow tail base

LENGTH 12 cm

LINNET

Acanthis cannabina

Linnets are not common visitors to gardens. They prefer open spaces such as heaths. Linnets are most likely to be seen in autumn, when they travel in flocks in search of weed seeds to feed on. Pairs of linnets can sometimes be seen in summer looking for suitable nesting sites.
VOICE The song is a soft, musical twitter and trill. Calls include a rapid trilling made in flight and a single "sooeet".
NEST Linnets nest in a variety of places, ranging from conifers and bushes to banks and grass tufts. *Nesting* April to August. 2 to 3 broods of 5 to 6 eggs. *Incubation* 11 to 13 days. *Fledging* 10 to 17 days.
ATTRACTED TO *Features* Hedges and shrubs, such as hawthorn and blackberry. *Natural foods* Seeds and insects. *Feeders* Rare visitors, but they may take grain and other seeds during harsh winter weather.

Female is dull brown, but male has red forehead and chest

Black and white wings

White-sided tail

LENGTH 13.5 cm

SISKIN

Carduelis spinus

Siskins are acrobatic finches, often feeding upside-down. The population of these birds has increased, due to new conifer plantations throughout Europe. Siskins are regular garden visitors, especially in wet weather when their preferred foods, conifer cones, are closed and conceal seeds.
VOICE The song is a soft mixture of jangly notes ending in a wheeze. The call notes are a "tsooee" and a twitter given on the wing.
NEST Siskins often build their nests at the ends of conifer branches. *Nesting* May to August. 1 to 2 broods of 3 to 5 eggs. *Incubation* 12 days. *Fledging* 15 days.
ATTRACTED TO *Features* Trees. *Natural foods* Cone seeds, especially those of birch, alder, and conifer, and insects. *Feeders* Regular visitors, taking peanuts, fat, and seeds.

LENGTH 16.5 cm

Males are mostly red; females are mostly green

Deeply cleft tail

COMMON CROSSBILL

Loxia curvirostra

Crossbills have unique, crossed bills that enable them to extract seeds from cones. Their nesting season is variable so that the birds can take advantage of ripening cone crops. As a result, local numbers of crossbills depend on the size of cone crops.
VOICE The song is a jerky sequence of "cheeree-cheeree-choop-chip-chip-chip-cheeree". The call note is a hard "jip jip" or "glip"
NEST Crossbills usually nest on high branches. *Nesting* January to May. 1 brood of 4 to 5 eggs. *Incubation* 13 to 16 days. *Fledging* 18 to 24 days.
ATTRACTED TO *Features* Conifers, thistles, berries, and water baths. *Natural foods* Cone seeds. *Feeders* Extremely rare visitors, taking seeds.

BULLFINCH

Pyrrhula pyrrhula

Bullfinches are shy birds that prefer to stay near woodland cover. They can be recognized by their large heads and stout bills. Their white rumps can often be glimpsed, just as the birds disappear into bushes. The severe damage that they cause to the buds and blossoms on fruit trees makes them unpopular visitors to fruit orchards.

VOICE The song is a quiet warble. The call is a whistling "deu-deu".

NEST Bullfinches prefer dense foliage and build their nests in thick hedges or conifers. *Nesting* April to August. 2 broods of 4 to 5 eggs. *Incubation* 14 days. *Fledging* 14 to 16 days.

ATTRACTED TO *Features* Lawns, budding fruit trees, willow, and weeds, especially nettles and dock. *Natural foods* Buds, seeds, and insects. *Feeders* Occasional visitors, taking peanuts and seeds.

Black crown

White wing bar and rump

Black tail

Bright pink underside

LENGTH 14.5 cm

REED BUNTING

Emberiza schoeniclus

Although they are mostly associated with fens and marshes, reed buntings are also common visitors to gardens and farmland, especially in winter. They will often join with flocks of finches or other seed-eating birds to feed. Reed buntings are named after their springtime habit of perching on the tops of reeds or bushes and bursting into song.

VOICE The song is a short, wheezing "zip-zip-zip-chittyk". The call note is a drawn-out "seee" and sounds similar to that of the yellow wagtail.

NEST Reed buntings generally choose well-hidden sites, in tussocks of grass or among bushes. *Nesting* April to August. 2 to 3 broods of 4 to 6 eggs. *Incubation* 14 days. *Fledging* 10 days.

ATTRACTED TO *Features* Lawns. *Natural foods* Seeds and insects. *Feeders* Occasional visitors, taking seeds.

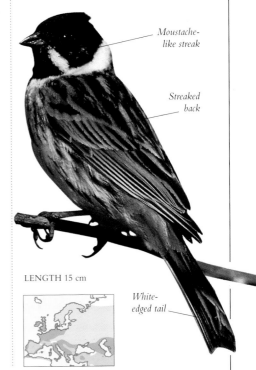

Moustache-like streak

Streaked back

LENGTH 15 cm

White-edged tail

LENGTH 17 cm

Conspicuous wing patch

White-tipped tail

HAWFINCH

Coccothraustes coccothraustes

Hawfinches are the second-largest European finches, after pine grosbeaks. They have large heads, and use their huge bills for cracking open cherry and plum stones to extract the kernels. Hawfinches are shy birds, but their presence can be ascertained from piles of shattered fruit stones found under trees.

VOICE The call note is a sharp "tick". The song comprises an unusual series of "ticks" and "jees"

NEST Hawfinches usually nest on horizontal branches of trees. *Nesting* April to June. 2 broods of 4 to 6 eggs. *Incubation* 12 days. *Fledging* 12 to 14 days.

ATTRACTED TO *Features* Fruit-bearing trees, such as hornbeam and sycamore. *Natural foods* Seeds, buds, and fruits. *Feeders* Occasional visitors, taking seeds and fruits.

Large bill cracks nuts

USEFUL ADDRESSES

Listed below are the addresses of useful points of contact for further information on the various horticultural topics and birdfeeding products covered in *Birdfeeder Garden*.

GARDENING ADVICE

The Royal Horticultural Society
80 Vincent Square,
London SW1P 2PE,
UNITED KINGDOM.

PLANT REFERENCE

The RHS Plant Finder is an annual publication that lists 65,000 plants and their sources.

Moorland Publishing Co. Ltd.
Moor Farm Road West,
Ashbourne, Derbyshire DE6 1HD,
UNITED KINGDOM.

ORGANIC HUSBANDRY

The Soil Association
Walnut Tree Manor, Haughley,
Stowmarket, Suffolk IP14 3RS,
UNITED KINGDOM.

WILDFLOWER SEEDS

**John Chambers'
Wild Flower Seeds**
15 Westleigh Road, Barton Seagrave,
Kettering, Northants NN15 5AJ,
UNITED KINGDOM.

FEEDERS, BIRDFOOD, NESTBOXES, AND RELATED ACCESSORIES

Jacobi Jayne & Company
Hawthorn Cottage, Maypole, Hoath,
Canterbury, Kent CT3 4LW,
UNITED KINGDOM.

BIRD CONSERVATION

**Bulgarian Society for
the Protection of Birds**
PO Box 114, Dianabad/Izgrev,
BG-1172 Sofia,
BULGARIA.

Czech Society for Ornithology
Hornam-Cholupská 34,
CZ-10200 Praha 10,
CZECH REPUBLIC.

Danish Ornithological Society
Fuglenes Hus, Vesterbrogade 140,
DK-1620 Copenhagen V,
DENMARK.

BirdLife Finland
PO Box 1285, FIN 00101 Helsinki,
FINLAND.

**Ligue pour la Protection
des Oiseaux**
La Corderie Royale, BP 263,
F-17305 Rochefort Cedex,
FRANCE.

**Naturschutzband
Deutschland e.V.**
Herbert-Rabius-Str. 26,
D-53225 Bonn,
GERMANY.

Hellenic Ornithogloical Society
Emm. Benaki 53, GR-106 81 Athens,
GREECE.

Birdwatch Ireland
Ruttledge House, 8 Longford Place,
Monkstown, Dublin,
IRELAND.

Lega Italiana Protezione Uccelli
Vicolo San Tiburzio 5,
I-43100 Parma,
ITALY.

Vogelbescherming Nederland
Driebergseweg 16c,
NL-3708 UB Zeist,
THE NETHERLANDS.

Norsk Ornithologisk Forening
Seminarplassen 5,
N-7060, Klæbu,
NORWAY.

**Polish Society for the
Protection of Birds**
PO Box 335,
PL-80-958 Gdansk 50,
POLAND.

Romanian Ornithological Society
Str. Republicii 48,
RO-3400 Cluj,
ROMANIA.

Russian Bird Conservation Union
110 Kibalchicha St 6, Building 5,
RUS-Moscow 129 278,
RUSSIA.

Sociedad Española de Ornitología
Carretera de Húmera No 63, 1,
E-28224 Pozuela de Alarcón,
Madrid,
SPAIN.

Swedish Ornithological Society
Ekshagsv 3,
S-10405 Stockholm,
SWEDEN.

Schweizer Vogelschutz
PO Box 8521, CH-8036 Zurich,
SWITZERLAND.

**Society for the Protection
of Nature**
PK 18,
TR-80810 Bebek-Istanbul,
TURKEY.

BirdLife International
Wellbrook Court, Girton Road,
Cambridge CB3 ONA,
UNITED KINGDOM.

**The Royal Society for the
Protection of Birds**
The Lodge, Sandy,
Bedfordshire SG19 2DL,
UNITED KINGDOM.

THE ROYAL SOCIETY FOR THE PROTECTION OF BIRDS

THE ROYAL SOCIETY FOR THE PROTECTION OF BIRDS (known as the RSPB) is a charity dependent on voluntary support. It actively protects the interests of wild birds and their environment, basing its actions upon good science and supported by the belief that birds and nature enrich people's lives. The RSPB also believes that nature conservation is fundamental to a healthy environment on which humans are dependent too.

One-quarter of the birds in the United Kingdom are declining – the RSPB would like to see this trend reversed, with a healthy countryside that is rich in birds and other wildlife. The charity is concerned with all wild birds, not just rare species, because even familiar birds such as the song thrush and skylark are in trouble. These birds need large areas of varied habitat, while others, such as the bittern and Dartford warbler, are so restricted to specific habitats that nature reserves can help protect them. The RSPB has more than 140 such reserves in the United Kingdom and manages about 100,000 hectares for the benefit of wildlife and people alike. Yet, it is keenly aware that gardens add up to a larger area than all of the nature reserves put together and play a huge part in wildlife conservation, for birds, frogs, hedgehogs, and much more.

The RSPB is also concerned about birds internationally, not least because most of the birds that are commonly seen in the United Kingdom spend many months each year overseas. Together with other bird welfare and conservation organizations, it has joined in a global partnership, BirdLife International, to strengthen the action taken internationally for the conservation of birds and their habitats.

The RSPB is not a political organization and has no party political bias; however, it lobbies government policy concerning, for example, agriculture, fisheries, drainage, and planning matters, all of which can directly affect birds and their natural habitats. The success of the charity depends on public backing and, for this reason, the RSPB strives to increase the size of its membership, which recently reached one million. These members offer the strength of their determined support as well as the finance for the charity to carry out its work.

One of the aims of the RSPB is to provide and encourage a greater understanding and appreciation of birds and their place in the world. To this end, the charity undertakes an extensive public information and educational role. It is committed to ensuring that young people, the decision-makers of the future, are well aware of the seriousness of the conservation challenge and the importance of success for the RSPB's work.

For details about membership of the RSPB, or if you would like more information about any aspect of the RSPB's work, please write to:

RSPB
The Lodge, Sandy,
Bedfordshire SG19 2DL.

INDEX

Bold page numbers refer to main entries in the text. *Italic* page numbers refer to illustrations.

ACKNOWLEDGMENTS

Dorling Kindersley and PAGE*One* would like to thank the following people: David Ashby for distribution map artworks; Sarah Brennan, RSPB, for editorial assistance; Chris Clark for DTP assistance; Gill Clarke for advice on garden design: Martine Collings for garden artworks; Jemima Dunne for initial work in planning this book; Peter Anderson, Peter Chadwick, Phillip Dowell, Neil Fletcher, Steve Gorton, Derek Hall, Jacqui Hurst, Dave King, Trevor Melton, Stephen Oliver, Kim Taylor, Matthew Ward, Stephen Wooster, and Jerry Young for special photography; Tim Hayward for bird artworks; D. P. Lee for making up the nestboxes; Chris Leon for advice on plant toxicity; Dave Miller for research assistance; Louise Thomas for picture research, and Sarah Young for woodcut illustrations.